# I HATE TAXES

Lower Your Taxes, Own Your Retirement

Joe F. Schmitz Jr.,
CFP®, ChFC®, CKA®

Expert Press
1067 N Main Street #235
Nicholasville, KY 40356
www.ExpertPress.net

# CONTENTS

# INTRODUCTION

*Anyone may arrange his affairs so that his taxes shall be as low as possible; he is not bound to choose that pattern which best pays the treasury. There is not even a patriotic duty to increase one's taxes.*

*Over and over again the Courts have said that there is nothing sinister in so arranging affairs as to keep taxes as low as possible. Everyone does it, rich and poor alike; and all do right, for nobody owes any public duty to pay more than the law demands.*

**Learned Hand (1872–1961), judge, US Court of Appeals**[1]

You know the old saying "It's not what you know but who you know"? Well, in my business of retirement planning, our saying is "It's not how much you *make*, it's how much you *keep*."

---

1    Gregory v. Helvering 69 F.2d 809, 810 (2d Cir. 1934), aff'd, 293 U.S. 465, 55 S.Ct. 266, 79 L.Ed. 596 (1935)

That's what this book is all about. You've worked hard all your life, but I can tell you without even knowing you or your situation that you're probably giving away much more of your hard-earned money to Uncle Sam than you need to. My job, my whole team's purpose, is to help you turn that around.

People are vastly different, but there's one thing we all have in common, no matter our background, age, race, gender, belief system, or profession:

---
**We all hate taxes.**
**And we all want to know how we can pay less.**

---

Don't get me wrong. I'll pay my fair share of taxes. I love this country, appreciate my citizenship, and will pay my taxes accordingly. I'm grateful for the opportunities I have in this country and the ease of life my family and I enjoy.

So let's be clear: We're not talking about "tax evasion," which means breaking the rules. We're talking about "tax avoidance," which means being smart about what the rules say. This is about knowing what tools the US Tax Code makes available to us, using them properly, and paying only our fair share. We would never encourage you to do things that would send you to jail.

As a US citizen, your tax avoidance is not only legal but necessary. It's your patriotic duty. The less you send to the government, the more you can spend and invest the way you choose and the more you can control. That could create jobs and wealth for our economy. I see saving money on taxes as a way to invest in America and make it a better place.

If I can legally understand what the tax code says and find loopholes to save money, then what do you think I'm going to do? I work hard for my money, and so do you. This is your life savings we're talking about. We need to be as diligent as possible to keep more money in your pocket and less in Uncle Sam's. Because guess what? He's not your real uncle.

Now, if you enjoy paying taxes and want to pay more, I'm afraid this book isn't for you. You would be better off staying status quo and sending in a donation to the IRS every year above what you pay in taxes. I'm also more than happy to give you a refund for this book.

This book—and all the planning my firm does for our clients—is about how to limit Uncle Sam's take from your pocket in retirement.

## My Three Goals for This Book

1. Motivate you to be proactive with your tax planning so that you have your own plan and not the IRS's plan.
2. Get you to the 0 percent tax bracket. This is what I call getting legally divorced from the IRS for life.
3. Save you potentially $100,000+ in tax planning.

Don't tip Uncle Sam. Pay your fair share but not a penny more—keep your hard-earned life savings in your pocket.

# CHAPTER 1

# WHY ACT NOW?

---

*Collecting more taxes than is absolutely necessary is legalized robbery.*

Calvin Coolidge, thirtieth president of the United States, 1923–1929

To express the duty that you must pay the least amount of taxes—only the amount you owe—I went to the IRS website. The Taxpayer Bill of Rights literally includes, "The Right to Pay No More than the Correct Amount of Tax."[2]

The right! I will exercise that right to pay no more than the correct amount of tax.

The *I Hate Taxes* book title comes from one of our clients—I'll call her Jeannie—after she chose to trust us with her life savings. It was one of those memorable moments you never forget. Jeannie stopped me cold near the start

---

2    https://www.irs.gov/taxpayer-bill-of-rights.

of our session and looked me dead in the eye. Her voice raised, she said to me, "Joe, there's one thing I want you to know about me. I hate taxes. I don't like anything about them. I don't like how they're spent, and I don't want to pay for things I disagree with. I want to pay the least amount possible. I want to spend my money on what matches my values and beliefs, and I don't trust the government."

She's right.

The other problem with taxes is that sometimes they don't make sense. For example, tax benefits are given to people who make a positive impact on the environment, such as buying an electric car. Yet people are also given a tax benefit for buying a gas-guzzling RV motorhome, which has the opposite impact. A popular tax benefit is charitable gifting, which I heartily agree with and love what it can do for our country, but other benefits are less clear. Who's making these rules? Which rules are best? What are we truly incentivizing? Do the incentives match your values? Not always the case for me.

# CHAPTER 2

# WE'RE DIFFERENT FROM OTHER PLANNERS

I've made it my mission—and the mission of our firm at Peak Retirement Planning, Inc.—to help people pay the least amount of taxes over their lifetime. Our mission differentiates us from the masses, as many financial planners and CPAs won't talk about tax planning at all.

---

**Tax planning isn't talked about enough.**

---

Why aren't taxes talked about? For many, they'll be their biggest expense over their lifetime. Why then won't financial planners and CPAs bring these strategies to the table for you? We'll discuss why this is the case in chapter 20, so stay tuned.

Everyone's situation is unique. Married or single. Dependents or not. Deductibles or none. Different incomes make what I'm about to cite challengeable, but here goes: Among the more than 164 million Americans who filed tax returns in 2020, the average federal income tax payment was $16,615, according to the most recent Internal Revenue Service data.[3]

Do the math over forty years of your active working life. That's $664,600. And that's an average of all tax-paying Americans. Ask yourself, did I even pay that much for my home? Not likely.

And still, many of you are scoffing, thinking that you've paid far more than that—and you would be right.

---

**Here's the real question to ask:
Did we need to pay that much?**

---

And here's the other question to ask: Are we truly paying our fair share?

If you review the following chart from the Tax Foundation website, it may show that you're paying well more than what others are paying. Fifty percent of taxpayers pay on average a 3.1 percent tax rate. I would imagine you're paying much more than that considering you're reading a book about hating taxes and saving money.

---

3    "How much income tax does the average American pay the IRS?" Liz Knueven, Business Insider, Updated February 1, 2023, https://www.businessinsider.com/personal-finance/average-federal-income-tax-payment-by-income.

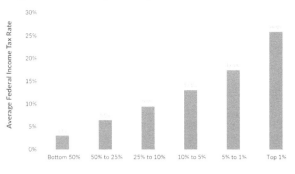

**High-Income Taxpayers Paid the Highest Average Income Tax Rates**

*Average Federal Income Tax Rate by Income Group, 2020*

Source: "Summary of the Latest Federal Income Tax Data," Erica York, January 26, 2023, https://taxfoundation.org/publications/latest-federal-income-tax-data/.

I agree with the biblical reference of Luke 12:48, "To whom much is given, much will be required," and so I'll pay my fair share. But is it fair to penalize people who work hard and save money and reward people who don't work hard or save money? I would rather save money on taxes that aren't always used for my personal convictions and instead use that tax savings toward what I feel can make a true impact in this world.

---

**If you hate taxes, don't avoid the IRS; instead, play their own game at an expert level.**

---

At Peak Retirement Planning, Inc., our experts know how to play (and win) the tax game. We know how to make an impact and help hardworking people keep their hard-earned life savings. Our firm delivers hundreds of workshops each year in our communities. We're constantly putting out content via our *Joe Knows Retirement* YouTube channel and podcast, TV, radio, articles featured in Kiplinger, and the books I write. I've seen too many people pay more taxes than they should, and we want to change that before it's too late.

During my years in financial planning, I've come to realize that there are two types of people who don't pay taxes: poor people and smart people. If you're poor, you reach a point where your income is so low that the government doesn't ask you for income taxes. If you're smart, you could live a tax-free retirement by understanding the rules and giving yourself enough time to plan. Being smart doesn't involve being poor.

We have a widowed client right now, Sarah, who has $1 million in her retirement accounts and will pay no more taxes for the rest of her life. This is what she and I call "legally divorcing the IRS for the rest of your life."

We can help many of our clients get to this spot. Sarah certainly isn't poor, but extremely smart financially. She has followed our advice over the years to get to where she needs to be. You may have heard that the rich also don't pay taxes. This annoys some, but I applaud them for being smart. The rich don't pay taxes because they hire smart people to show them strategies to reduce their taxes. Maybe you should do that yourself.

It's not what you know but who you know, right? Not only that: It isn't how much you make, it's how much you keep.

---

**In short, when it comes to the rich, don't hate the player, hate the game.**

---

There are loopholes in the US Tax Code for everyone— if you're smart enough to find them.

And, if like Sarah you have over $1 million net worth, then you're in the top 10 percent of our country's wealth.[4] Hate it or love it, you're wealthy. And most of your wealth is in tax-deferred investments with your partner Uncle Sam.

You better get busy planning. Hundreds of thousands of your dollars are on the line. If you're a saver and have done the right thing, then you're being desensitized. The tax system has penalized savers and benefited non-savers. That's criminal, if you ask me. The IRS can change the rules on us at any time.

## Change Is Hard

Sometimes we know we need to change, and we don't want to. For some, you might know you need to eat healthily, but

---

4    "33 Incredible Millionaire Statistics [2023]: 8.8% of US Adults Are Millionaires," Abby McCain, February 24, 2023, https://www.zippia.com/advice/millionaire-statistics/.

you would rather go for the dessert, or you might know you need to get off your phone or social media, but you can't because you're addicted.

When it comes to taxes (and other things), inaction is the worst kind of action. The biggest advice I can give you through this book is to *get help*. The US Tax Code is complex. There are more words in the tax code than the Bible. Do you know what all the words mean? Have you ever even read it? If not, you're at risk of losing money and susceptible to government control, with less money in your pocket long term.

I cover tax-planning strategies in this book and will try to make them seem easy, but understand there is much more to it, and I'm only providing general information. Everyone's situation is specific, and everything I say in this book will be different for different people.

In my life, I try to delegate everything I'm not an expert at. I go to a doctor to perform surgery on me, I go to a mechanic to change my oil, and I have a team clean my house. I'm not good at cleaning, and I don't want to spend five hours on a Saturday doing it. I would rather spend my Saturdays writing tax books.

My point is, are you really going to have the time to understand how to make the smartest decisions financially with a full-time job, family responsibilities, hobbies, and other obligations? From what I see, that's a recipe for disaster. If you're not on top of tax planning, you could miss saving hundreds of thousands of dollars over your lifetime. My goal with this book is to create a paradigm shift. Everyone is telling you not to pay taxes, but I'm going to tell you to pay your taxes now so you don't have to pay them later.

## The IRS's Plan or Your Plan?

You have a decision to make. You can follow the status quo and ignore the opportunities at your fingertips—what we would consider the IRS's plan. The IRS's plan could cost you lots of money in mistakes over time as discussed earlier. Or you can follow your own plan where you know what's being done and when it's being done. Your plan could save you money on taxes. At the end of the day, your actions will decide your financial future.

After reading this book, talk with us at Peak Retirement Planning, Inc. The book is meant to open your eyes and prod you into action as you learn about basic and advanced strategies that may be a good fit for your circumstances. We're here for you.

# CHAPTER 3

# KICK UNCLE SAM TO THE CURB

I want to challenge you to think through *why* you are reading this book. The more money you have, the more important your reasons.

It's great to save lots of money and avoid giving it to Uncle Sam, but . . . why? Why are you saving money? Is it for fun? Is it for the satisfaction of winning the money game? If so, that's great and I applaud you.

> **My point is for you to think intentionally about the money you've worked so hard for.**

I think you can dig deep and find more value and impact for the money you have and are accumulating. Here's the deal: You can't take this money with you. You can't pull a U-Haul filled with money behind your hearse.

Whatever your situation, my challenge to you is the same: Determine where your money would be best used based on your values, life goals, and deepest wishes. You can only do a few things with your money.

## Give to Yourself—Spend It All

First, you can spend your money. You may even want to start spending more money before it's too late. One of the best pieces of advice I've received from our clients is "Travel and do the things you want to do *now*, because the older you get, the harder it gets."

Maybe that means buying items at the store when they aren't on sale or not driving across town to save a few cents on gas. It may mean going on a trip you've dreamed about but didn't want to spend the money.

We once had a client who saved over $1 million and had pensions and Social Security that were more than enough to live the lifestyle he wanted to in retirement. We told him he had enough to cover his "paychecks" and that his investments were considered his "playchecks." This meant he could spend his investments however he pleased for the fun stuff. That triggered a thought, and he suddenly started to name off things he wanted to do that he never thought he could because he was always worried about having enough.

He said, "I want a pool in the basement and an infrared sauna to improve my health. I want to go on a cruise once a month, and I want to fly first class." After we ran the numbers, all his ideas fit within his playcheck budget. The annual planning sessions we have with him now are so much more fruitful for both of us. We get to see the pictures of his trips, see his health improve with a loss of over fifty pounds, and see the joy he feels on his glowing face. It makes what we do that much more purposeful.

However, I've met with more than one client who has said, "I want to leave money to my children." That's the old-school, traditional way of doing things: working your fingers to the bone to develop wealth during your active life, living well in retirement, and leaving a significant residual amount of money to the children.

But maybe the children have plenty of income and are saving and investing. They tell Mom and Dad, "We don't need your money. Live well and spend it all on yourself." This is what I tell my parents. They've already given me the best gifts I could ask for. I would rather they enjoy their money than me.

Don't get caught thinking you can't enjoy everything you've worked hard for. We find many of our clients spend more money in retirement. We often work with the millionaire next door. The person who has saved like crazy, has been frugal, and doesn't have all the fancy belongings. It's hard for them to spend money; they've spent their lifetime *not* spending. My third book *Midwestern Millionaire* is all about the dreams, needs, and challenges these people face. Also, that's their identity, and spending money gives them anxiety. I get it. I'm the same way. But know that if all your retirement goals are met, you have permission to enjoy it and spend it. If you don't want to spend it all, there are other options.

## Give to Your Family

Second, you can give your money to your family. If this is your goal, I would ask you to think about whether this is the best place for your money. I'm not saying it isn't. That's up to you to decide.

Here's a little-known fact: Studies have found that 70% of the time, family assets are lost from one generation to the next.[5] Inheritances are spent right away because the money is found money, not earned money. It's like winning the lottery. Other studies also show that winning the lottery

---

5    "5 Strategies to Keep Your Heirs From Blowing Their Inheritance," Anna Kates Smith, October 02, 2015.

is one of the worst things that can happen to you. I've seen instances in our practice where leaving behind an inheritance ruined lives.

It may sound like I'm talking you out of giving money to family, but I'm not. It's a good idea to leave an inheritance if done the right way. I think it's a responsibility for families to leave a lasting impact for generations to come. One of my goals is to provide enough financial resources for future Schmitz generations so they have more opportunities without worrying about funds.

One way to give to your loved ones is to give while you are living so you can see where the money is going. If you do decide to leave money to family or friends, I recommend you have a conversation with them about what it will look like to express your values and what you would like them to do with it.

You could also give money to your grandchildren to help them buy a home or car, start a business, pay for higher or specific education, or get started in building wealth.

You could even investigate more advanced ways of using trusts to give income streams that can last for generations to come—in other words, provide generational wealth to your family like I'm doing.

## Give to Charity

Third, you can give all or part of your money to a charity and make a significant impact in our world. Leaving a generous amount of $10,000 to $1 million (or more) would have a lasting impact on a charity of your choice and the success of their mission.

I tell people that this type of gift is how you leave a legacy. The receiving organization might put a picture of you in their building, name a building after you, or even put a statue of you out front. A way for your legacy to live on.

For our clients who are Christians and Kingdom-minded, we discuss "leaving the money to the kingdom" or "giving to the kingdom now." Psalm 24:1 says that God owns it all. This is where our Certified Kingdom Advisor (CKA®) credential comes into play for those interested in this type of planning. The strategies in this book can allow you to give more to the kingdom and less to Uncle Sam.

## Give to Uncle Sam

Fourth, you can leave a bequest to Uncle Sam, also known as . . . taxes.

Do any of you have Uncle Sam as a beneficiary on your 401(k) account? He could be if you don't make changes now. What do I mean? Keep reading and find out. Inaction names Uncle Sam as your heir by default. But I know all of you will act, and this won't be an option.

---

**Plan ahead. Plan now. Plan well.**

---

# CHAPTER 4

# WILL TAXES GO UP OR DOWN?

## Current National Debt

Go to USDebtClock.org to see the current amount of debt in our country right now.

Watching that clock gives me anxiety. That amount of debt is hard to grasp.

Our country has well over $36 trillion in debt, and it's growing every day. To put this number in perspective, I'll write it out numerically to give you maximum visual impact: $36,000,000,000,000. When you say the number out loud, it doesn't ring any alarm bells, but when you see it written out—it's a serious number. If you're still struggling to grasp how big of a number $30 trillion is, I'll break it down this way:

How big is $1 trillion?

If $1 equals 1 second, then $1 million equals 11½ days.

That means $1 billion equals 32 years.

That means $1 trillion equals 32,000 years. Our country owes thirty times this. Yikes.

To put it another way: Go back a billion seconds, and you would be in the 1990s. Go back a trillion seconds, and you would be around 30,000 BC.[6]

This is a massive amount of debt. I recommend everyone watch *The Power of Zero*. This documentary discusses our current debt crisis and interviews experts on the topic and what their research and expertise tell us about the outlook of our country. It presents the concept that tax rates would have to double over the next ten years to be able to pay off this debt. Double! This is a simple math equation. It doesn't matter who's in political office; it's what the numbers tell us.

Does that show you how serious this is?

To solve the debt crisis, there are only so many things that can happen. Let me simplify it for you:

1. The government can raise taxes.
2. The government can reduce spending.

Those are the options. Not too many people think the government will reduce spending, considering the amount

---

6    "How much is $1 trillion? Well, Apple could buy everyone in San Francisco an apartment," Ryan Suppe, USA Today, Updated September 1, 2018, https://www.usatoday.com/story/tech/talkingtech/2018/08/02/how-comprehend-trillion-dollars/890715002/.

of money they've spent and are planning to spend, so that leaves us with raising taxes.

There is a third path: The government could raise inflation. I consider inflation a hidden tax. Who's most affected by inflation? Retirees on a fixed income.

What is inflation? Inflation is when the government prints more money, which forces the cost of goods to increase. For example, if you went to the store for a dozen eggs in the 1970s, it cost you around one dollar. Today, you may have to pay over four dollars on average. That's inflation in a nutshell.

I consider it "basic" to understand how much debt the nation has and how much income it has. If you're running a household or running a business, these are the basic numbers you would want to know, right? If you use credit cards, you want to know that your outstanding balance is less than your income so that you can pay off the credit card balance every month. Basic household finance. Yet so many legislators blow this off when it comes to managing the finances of our nation. Citizens don't think they can do anything about this information (and that is somewhat but not entirely true, as you will see in these pages).

We need to ask ourselves, Is the government really being the best steward of our tax-paying dollars? The thing that frustrates me is that the government is under no disciplinary checks-and-balances system when they overspend.

If you go to the store with nothing in your bank account, what do you walk out with? Nothing. If the government goes to the store with nothing in their bank account, what do they walk out with? Everything. Is that fair?

Only time will tell what the future has in store.

But knowing about the nation's debt and current situation will set you up for understanding your own tax picture.

CHAPTER 5

# THE NITTY-GRITTIES

My mentor and best friend, Kathy Gilliland, a retired financial advisor of thirty-nine years, is the person who got me into the industry and is one of the biggest influences on my life. Without her, Peak Retirement Planning, Inc. wouldn't exist, and neither would this book. One of the best tips she gave me over the years was to always explain financial concepts at a fourth-grade level. Not everyone enjoys this stuff. In honor of her, that is my goal for this book, and especially this chapter: to get across the basic understanding of how taxes work.

There are two interesting and basic concepts that I always like our clients to understand at the start of any conversation. The first is the concept of the marginal tax bracket. The second is the concept of the standard deduction.

# Understanding the Marginal Tax Bracket

| FEDERAL INCOME TAX RATES 2025 | | |
|---|---|---|
| RATE | SINGLE FILERS | MARRIED FILING JOINTLY |
| 10% | $0-$11,925 | $0-$23,850 |
| 12% | $11,925-$48,475 | $23,850-$96,950 |
| 22% | $48,475-$103,350 | $96,950-$206,700 |
| 24% | $103,350-$197,300 | $206,700-$394,600 |
| 32% | $197,300-$250,525 | $394,600-$501,050 |
| 35% | $250,525-$626,350 | $501,050-$751,600 |
| 37% | $626,350+ | $751,600+ |

Source Adapted from: http://taxfoundation.org/2025-tax-brackets/.

The preceding chart displays the 2025 tax-rate table on taxable income. This chart only considers federal taxes.

This is where most of the nation's tax revenue comes from, so let's make sure we understand it clearly. Each line on the chart is a *marginal* tax rate and not a *flat* tax rate.

That's what many people don't understand. What these percentages represent is one of the biggest misconceptions we see with taxes.

A married filing jointly taxpayer would go to the chart to find their $100,000 annual income and assume they must pay a full 22 percent on their $100,000.

That's not how it works, and thank goodness.

We had a client who thought this. His taxable income was $94,000, and he was married filing jointly. He was happy to find himself in the 12 percent bracket. But there

26

was sand in the machine: He had the option of receiving a $5,000 bonus from work and turned it down. Why? He thought that money would bump his total income to $99,000 and therefore into the 22 percent bracket. He thought he would have to pay 10 percent more on his total $99,000 income. He was wrong. Only the $2,050 above that limit (the amount of new income above the $96,950 of the 12 percent bracket) would be taxable at 22 percent, and the rest would be at the lower brackets. He should have taken the bonus.

## Understanding the Standard Deduction

Now let's understand how the standard deduction plays a part here. The amount of income up to the top of the standard deduction is tax-free.

How much is that deduction? It varies from year to year, and here's what it looks like for 2023:

| STANDARD DEDUCTION & PERSONAL EXEMPTION | |
| --- | --- |
| FILING STATUS | DEDUCTION AMOUNT |
| Single | $15,000 |
| Married | $30,000 |
| Head of Household | $22,500 |

Source: http://taxfoundation.org/2025-tax-brackets/.

If your income stays under these amounts in 2023, you won't have to pay tax. Great deal.

To clarify, if your income is only $30,000 and you are married filing jointly, then you pay zero—nothing—in taxes that year.

So how do we get your income down to that point, without eating ramen noodles every day? The key is to be able to show a lower income for your retirement years. We'll share an example later in this book about clients of ours who live on $100,000 per year, but they're able to show their income under $30,000 because several of their income sources are tax-free. We discuss this concept throughout the book.

Currently, over 90 percent of people take the standard deduction with the current tax code. The standard deduction is so high that most people don't manage to itemize deductions higher (they just don't have that much to deduct) than that amount.

Now, that hasn't always been the case—and it probably won't be in the future. When the Tax Cuts and Jobs Act expires, more people will itemize when the standard deduction gets cut nearly in half, and other itemized deductions that had gone away will be brought back.

---

**It's hard to overemphasize how generous the standard deduction is right now.**

---

So, back to the brackets and marginal tax rates.

After the standard deduction, you now enter the 10 percent tax bracket. In this bracket you will only pay 10 percent tax on the next $23,850 (if you are married filing jointly). Then you enter the 12 percent bracket, where you will then only pay 12 percent tax on the amount of your income that falls within that bracket. I think you get the point as that concept applies for each bracket. That's how a marginal tax bracket works.

## The Widow's Penalty

Before we move on from the brackets, I want to point out a huge planning opportunity if you are married filing jointly on taxes. If one spouse passes away, then you now must file as a single in the year following death (unless you have dependents, then you have a couple more years to do tax planning, which you'll most likely want to put to good use). This is called the "widow's penalty."

If you follow the chart with the tax brackets, you'll see that the brackets are nearly cut in half, although the widow's income is typically about the same as it was when married. The spouse's investments would go over to them, and so they would still have the same amount of impact from that. They would also likely have a survivor option if they had a pension. The only thing that would differ would be a loss in one spouse's Social Security.

To prove this point, look at the tax brackets and see that if you're married and your taxable income is $85,000, then all of that income is at 12 percent. However, if you're single with the same amount of income, then your $85,000 of taxable income would turn into almost $100,000 of income because of a reduced standard deduction. On top of that bad news, the majority of your income now falls (again, as a single filer) in the 22 percent bracket.

That means you're paying nearly double the taxes. You're paying almost $10,000 more in taxes on the same amount of income. Yikes.

This is where planning is important.

Knowing that one spouse is going to predecease the other (and it almost always happens that way), this is something you need to be planning for before it's too late. Use the lower tax rates while you have them.

While we typically see this when one spouse isn't expected to live as long, this planning opportunity might also be based on age and statistically understanding that females live longer than males. Do you want your spouse to be subject to higher rates on the condensed single brackets?

To really drive this widow's tax concept home, I want to show you a picture of a gentleman who will always have a soft place in my heart.

This is Uncle Chuck. The photo was taken at a client appreciation event we had for our clients at a nice steak house. As you can see, Uncle Chuck is wearing overalls. You might think that his choice of clothing isn't appropriate for an event like this, but around me, Uncle Chuck got to do whatever he wanted. He has been there with me since day one. Uncle Chuck was my first client when I got into the financial planning industry. That level of trust obviously means a lot to me.

This picture was taken six months before his death. The good news is we were able to do tax planning before he passed away so that he could leave my Aunt Terri in a better position. We used the married filing jointly brackets so Aunt Terri wouldn't have to worry about "showing" higher income in her single filing tax years.

To close out this story, I want to go back to December 2022 when Uncle Chuck wasn't doing too well. I was meeting with him to review everything financially. I knew how much he appreciated distinctions, so I told him straight up, "If you make it to at least January 2023, then you'll allow your wife to be in a much better situation. We'll be able to use the more advantageous married filing jointly tax brackets for 2023. If you pass today, she would have to file with the less generous single tax brackets for 2023."

Strange conversation? Not with Uncle Chuck. He got it. And sure enough, Uncle Chuck made it to January 2023 before he passed away. I knew with his love for his wife and desire to make sure she was going to be all right, that challenge was going to be fulfilled, and sure enough it was.

I may be biased (okay, I *am* biased), but Uncle Chuck was way tougher than Uncle Sam. To prove it, Uncle Chuck beat Uncle Sam in the tax fight.

# CHAPTER 6

# TAXES ARE ON SALE

The current debt crisis leads me to be concerned about legislative risk.

When people come in to see us, we always ask them, "What is your biggest concern in retirement?" Every time, by far, the answer is "running out of money."

Running out of their own money is a concern for about 99 percent of the world's population. Because if you have $1 million, then what do you want? You want $2 million. And if you have $2 million, what do you want? You want $4 million. And if you have $4 million, what do you want? $8 million. Once you have $8 million, you're no longer afraid of running out of money—or so I've heard. Reality check. That $8 million mark is in the hands of less than 1 percent of our population.

Remember what I've already said:
It's not how much you make,
it's how much you keep.

Along with most people's "running out of money" worries, a substantial risk in retirement that can cause this is, in my opinion, legislative risk.

## Legislative Risk

Here's why legislative risk is worrisome: If you have large tax-deferred investments or accounts, such as 401(k)s or individual retirement accounts (IRAs), you haven't paid taxes on any of that money yet. But at some point in the future, you'll have to, which is the case for most of our clients when they first start working with us.

But how much in taxes will you have to pay? That's the tricky part. You don't know what Congress will do in the next five, ten, or twenty years that will affect your tax picture. Legislative risk.

Now it's true that current tax rates are near a historical low. Look at the following chart, and you see that this year, the top rate is "just" 37 percent. However, in 1981, the top tax rate was 70 percent. After World War II, the top tax rate on the chart was at 94 percent.

# Taxing The Rich: How America's Marginal Tax Rate Evolved

Historic highest marginal income tax rates in the U.S.*

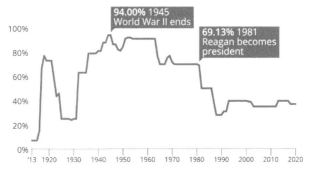

94.00% 1945
World War II ends

69.13% 1981
Reagan becomes
president

* Marginal tax rate is the highest tax rate paid on someone's income and only
applies to income over a certain level. - e.g. earnings above $200,000 in 1960
were taxed at 90%.
Source: Tax Policy Center

statista 🅩

In the past, people weren't motivated to make a lot of money. For example, actors (like Ronald Reagan) would make two movies and call it quits for the year. If they made more movies and therefore more income, they would get to keep little to none of the extra earnings. Plus, they would still have to pay other taxes, such as state taxes.

It's the old argument about working more for the government than yourself.

I know not everyone falls into that higher bracket, but when you look back at historical rates, the highest bracket is a good indicator that the lower brackets will be higher as well.

Look at the following chart from 1981, which our team put together with careful research. If you have $85,000 taxable income today, then you're in the 12 percent bracket. We saw this earlier in the current chart. If you have that same taxable income today, and you're suddenly taxed at the 1981 rates, you're in the 32 percent bracket. What a jump! Not double, but almost triple.

| 1981 TAX BRACKETS (INFLATION ADJUSTED)[7] MARRIED FILING JOINTLY | |
| --- | --- |
| Marginal Tax Rate | Tax Brackets |
| 0% | $0–$11,412 |
| 14% | $11,413–$18,463 |
| 16% | $18,464–$25,513 |
| 18% | $25,514–$39,948 |
| 21% | $39,949–$53,712 |
| 24% | $53,713–$67,811 |
| 28% | $67,812–$82,582 |

---

7    "Value of 1981 US Dollars today," Inflation Tool, https://www.inflationtool.com/us-dollar/1981-to-present-value?amount=7600&year2=2023&frequency=yearly; "Historical U.S. Federal Individual Income Tax Rates & Brackets, 1862-2021," Tax Foundation, August 24, 2021, https://taxfoundation.org/historical-income-tax-rates-brackets/. Accessed July 2023.

| 1981 TAX BRACKETS (INFLATION ADJUSTED)[7] MARRIED FILING JOINTLY | |
|---|---|
| Marginal Tax Rate | Tax Brackets |
| 32% | $82,583–$100,375 |
| 37% | $100,376–$118,167 |
| 43% | $118,168–$153,752 |
| 49% | $153,753–$201,422 |
| 54% | $201,423–$287,363 |
| 59% | $287,364–$367,260 |
| 64% | $367,261–$545,184 |
| 68% | $545,185–$723,108 |
| 70% | $723,109+ |

Source: https://taxfoundation.org/data/all/federal/historical-income-tax-rates-brackets/#:~:text=%2441%2C500-,1981,-0.0%25.

I know this is a hard question, but would you rather pay 12 percent or 32 percent? These rates aren't set to come back, but what do you think could happen in the future knowing what we know?

---

**Our current low tax rates are why I say, "Taxes are on sale."**

---

Plan now before it's too late.

We don't know what tax rates will be for certain in the future. But fifteen or twenty years in the future is going to be your lifetime. Many of our clients are just entering retirement. They're in their early to late sixties. We have no idea what the US tax brackets will look like when they're in their early to late eighties.

We know that legislative risk will be present in the near future when the Tax Cuts and Jobs Act expires. You may recall that what this did (TCJA) was lower tax rates; it started in 2018.

The key is to start planning *now*.

If your advisor hasn't emphasized to you what's going to happen when these tax cuts expire—and hasn't shown you ways to plan for it since 2018—then you may want to consider if your advisor specializes in tax planning.

Unfortunately, we see this far too often from people who meet with us looking for a different relationship. They tell us they do not want to miss opportunities and leave money on the table any longer.

Right now, tax rates are on sale. For a limited time. Plan now. Take advantage of the fact before the sale ends.

Study the following chart to see the impact we're talking about here.

- If you're in the 12 percent bracket now, in 2023, you would have been in the 15 percent bracket back in 2017.
- If you're in the 22 percent bracket now, you would have been in the 25 percent bracket in 2017.

- If you're in the 24 percent bracket now, you would have been in the 28 percent bracket in 2017.

Which rate would you rather pay? Are taxes on sale right now? You get to choose what rates you want to pay your taxes at.

### FEDERAL INCOME TAX RATES 2025

| RATE | SINGLE FILERS | MARRIED FILING JOINTLY |
|---|---|---|
| 10% | $0-$11,925 | $0-$23,850 |
| 12% | $11,925-$48,475 | $23,850-$96,950 |
| 22% | $48,475-$103,350 | $96,950-$206,700 |
| 24% | $103,350-$197,300 | $206,700-$394,600 |
| 32% | $197,300-$250,525 | $394,600-$501,050 |
| 35% | $250,525-$626,350 | $501,050-$751,600 |
| 37% | $626,350+ | $751,600+ |

### STANDARD DEDUCTION & PERSONAL EXEMPTION

| FILING STATUS | DEDUCTION AMOUNT |
|---|---|
| Single | $15,000 |
| Married | $30,000 |
| Head of Household | $22,500 |

Source: http://taxfoundation.org/2025-tax-brackets/.

## FEDERAL INCOME TAX RATES 2017

| RATE | SINGLE FILERS | MARRIED FILING JOINTLY |
|---|---|---|
| 10% | $0-$9,325 | $0-$18,650 |
| 15% | $9,326-$37,950 | $18,651-$75,900 |
| 25% | $37,951-$91,900 | $75,901-$153,100 |
| 28% | $91,901-$191,650 | $153,101-$233,350 |
| 33% | $191,651-$416,700 | $233,351-$416,700 |
| 35% | $416,701-$418,400 | $416,701-$470,700 |
| 39.6% | $418,401+ | $470,701+ |

## STANDARD DEDUCTION & PERSONAL EXEMPTION

| FILING STATUS | DEDUCTION AMOUNT |
|---|---|
| Single | $6,350 |
| Married | $12,700 |
| Head of Household | $9,350 |

Source: https://taxfoundation.org/data/all/federal/historical-income-tax-rates-bracket
s/#:~:text=%24500%2C000-,2017,-10.0%25.

## Blueberries

My family is frugal, and we love saving money. It's a joke at times. I was raised that way, and it has become a way of life for us. Don't get me wrong. We live well. We just don't live wastefully.

We'll stick to better-value restaurants rather than the fancy, high-end, overpriced ones. We won't buy loads of material things and certainly not anything considered flashy.

Let me share my beloved blueberry story to emphasize what I'm saying. I love blueberries, and as you now know I love saving money. So when I go to the store and blueberries are on sale, what do you think I do? Stock up, of course. My entire freezer is full when there's a blueberry sale. I know I'm going to use them—I put blueberries in my smoothie every day. Why would I go to the store a week later and pay double the price?

Like the blueberries, when "taxes are on sale" (as they are right now), buy now at the lower price. The amount you'll save is way better than any blueberry sale.

If you're like me and enjoy saving money, then taking advantage of this tax sale through smart planning will be apt to save you more money than any other strategy.

If you're the type who uses coupons at the store or drives across town to save a dime on gas, but you don't take advantage of this fire sale on taxes, you're leaving money on the table and not being tax smart.

Proper, informed, smart tax planning can save you hundreds of thousands of dollars. And it would probably take as much time as it would driving across town for that cheaper gas.

Wouldn't you be more interested in saving a couple of thousand dollars rather than a couple of bucks? So why are you not doing this?

The good news: You can act now.

# CHAPTER 7

# THE TAX-DEFERRED BUCKET

Everyone has a sizable portion of their saved money in the tax-deferred bucket. All your life you've been shoveling money into this bucket. This includes your 401(k), 403(b), IRA, 457, thrift savings plan (TSP), pensions, and any other employer-sponsored retirement account you may have.

Over 30 trillion American workers' dollars are in this bucket.

Why do we call it "tax-deferred"? You have put pretax dollars (also known as money you haven't yet paid taxes on) in this bucket. What we tend to forget, and therefore not plan for, is that at some point in the future you must pay taxes on this money.

So, is a tax-deferred bucket of investments a good deal? Seems like a good deal for the IRS and not for you. Here's why: If you put $10,000 into your tax-deferred investment, and over your working years it grows to $50,000, you would have to pay tax on $50,000. However, you've only received tax benefits on the initial $10,000. I don't know about you, but for me that's hard to feel good about. My question to you is, At what tax rate will you pay on this money?

Say you would have had to pay 15 percent on that initial $10,000 if you had not put it into a tax-deferred account. Fast forward thirty-five years when you want to withdraw (called "taking a distribution") from the account, and the tax rate due on the withdrawal might be 10 percent. It could just as well be 20 percent. I don't have a crystal ball, and neither do you.

With any tax-deferred investment, we're putting our trust in Uncle Sam that tax rates will be lower in the future (or at least no higher) than when we invested the money. Today, with tax rates on sale, this may not seem like such an urgent item to plan for.

But remember: On all tax-deferred investments, Uncle Sam is your business partner unless you do something about it. Also remember: When your 401(k) account statement tells you that you have $1 million, you must look yourself in the mirror and say, "No, I don't."

Uncle Sam is absolutely going to take his cut. That cut is whatever tax rate applies at the time you pull that money out of the account.

## How Much Money Do You Really Have?

I once had a gentleman come into our office to talk about his retirement. He said, "Joe, I have a million dollars, and I'm ready to retire." He showed me his 401(k) statement, and sure enough, it had his name and $1 million on it. But I had to tell him what I just told you: "Uncle Sam is your partner for life."

That means, no, he doesn't have $1 million for retirement.

He only has that amount in an account that is *co-owned by Uncle Sam.*

He has much less than $1 million when he factors in Uncle Sam's cut—aka taxes.

How much should we factor in for taxes, given that we don't know what the rates will be in fifteen or thirty years? Your guess is as good as mine; tax rates are written in pencil.

I like to think about it this way. My dad has raised me to be a businessman and to do things the right way. He never told me it was a good idea to go into business with someone who puts no work into the business, yet when it comes time to sell the business, they can get whatever percentage they desire. That's not fair. But this is what's happening with your tax-deferred investment. Uncle Sam is your business partner, and he's going to be there until you change it or until you take the money out. Would you rather do it now or later?

## Shopping without Looking

Have you ever gone to the grocery store and thrown whatever you see into your cart without looking at the price? I've never done this. Why? I'm frugal (as I've admitted) and want to save as much money as possible. I'm consistently looking for sales.

If you shop without looking, what price will you pay for your groceries that week? You have no idea. I guarantee, however, that you'll pay more than you needed to.

Well, if you have a tax-deferred investment, then you're shopping without looking. As I mentioned, the tax code is written in pencil. We have no idea what tax rates will be in the future. Right now, you're pushing your investment cart, which has a significant amount in it, and it's all in a tax-deferred investment. When you put money into this tax-deferred cart, you pay no taxes, but one day you'll pull up to the register, and you'll have to pay taxes on it when you check out. What tax rate will you pay? How much will your actual tax bill be?

We have no idea. We're trusting Uncle Sam not to raise taxes. We're trusting Uncle Sam will be nice to us in the future.

A study from PEW shows that trust in the government was at 75 percent around 1960, and now it's only around 25 percent.[8] I don't know about you, but I don't want to put my trust in Uncle Sam and our future outlook with the debt crisis we're in. I would rather see you take control and own your retirement.

## Not All Bad News

I know it seems I'm bashing you if you have this type of investment, but here's where I pat you on the back and inform you that you made a good decision if you have this investment.

You saw the chart from 1981. I showed you where the highest tax rate was 70 percent. Well, today, the highest tax rate is 37 percent. If you're good at math, then you can understand the difference between saving 70 percent back then and paying 37 percent now. That's a good deal.

---

**However, I must repeat: You must make sure you take advantage of the current tax sale before it passes you by.**

---

8    https://www.pewresearch.org/politics/2022/06/06/public-trust-in-government-1958-2022/. Accessed July 2023.

The "golden tax rule" is to defer taxes when they're high and pay them when they're low. So understand you've done your job, but now it's time for a change. The window is closing, but there's still time.

# CHAPTER 8

# THE TAX-FREE BUCKET

The tax-free bucket is where a lot of people wish to be, but they don't know how to get there.

We're referring to the Roth accounts in this bucket, which consist of accounts like Roth IRA, Roth 401(k), Roth 403(b), Roth TSP, etc.

I'll be spilling a lot of ink on those Roth accounts in these pages. Why? We want you to divorce Uncle Sam and live a tax-free retirement.

## Roth Basics

In a Roth IRA investment, you get no tax deduction up front. You must pay taxes on the money you deposit in this account—not great, I agree.

However, you get tax-free growth forever after that and never have to pay tax on that investment again. That is great.

For example, if you contribute $10,000 to this investment, then that will be after-tax money you've put into it. You already paid tax on it. Thus, you get no tax savings upfront like those tax-deferred investments. But when it grows to $50,000, and you take it all out, then you'll pay *no tax* on this money.

To make it clear, you paid tax on $10,000 and received $40,000 of growth with *no tax* associated with it. Who is that a good deal for? You, of course. Not Uncle Sam. We love that.

---

**So if we had a magic wand, where do we want all our money? The tax-free bucket.**

---

However, in dollar terms today, the tax-free investment is the smallest of the buckets. Less than 1 trillion of American savers' dollars are held in this bucket. According to the Investment Company Institute, less than 20 percent of people even have a Roth IRA.

There are many reasons why this is the case. Lack of education is the main one. Many don't understand the benefits of a Roth IRA or were never explained how it works. Educators don't teach this at schools, reporters don't talk about it on the news, and your family probably doesn't discuss it around the dinner table (unless you're part of my family). Even CPAs and most financial planners don't talk about this. So unless you're proactive or have a great mentor, you may not know about Roth IRAs.

This is why we at Peak Retirement Planning, Inc. are so passionate about education in our community about the power of Roth IRAs, especially in retirement.

Another reason people don't have as much money in a Roth investment account is because Roths haven't been around forever. The Roth IRA started in 1997, and the Roth 401(k) wasn't introduced until 2006. There are still companies that don't offer a Roth option. Most companies are offering it now, but it took them a while to introduce it. As a result you haven't had as much time to contribute to this investment.

Also, if you make too much money, then you can't contribute to a Roth IRA. You can potentially do something called a backdoor Roth IRA, which I do every year. Not everyone can do it, so you need to be careful about this.

Then, you must have earned income to contribute to a Roth IRA. If you're retired, then you can't contribute to a Roth IRA. If you're married, you can contribute to a Roth IRA if you're not working, but your spouse must be working.

And then, there are limits on how much you contribute. For example, for 2025, you can only contribute $7,000 a year if you're under age fifty, and $8,000 if you're over age fifty, due to the catch-up provision. You can take out those contributions at any time without tax or penalties. For Roth IRA contributions, you have until April 15 to contribute for the prior year.

For the Roth 401(k), you can only contribute $23,500 under age fifty. People ages fifty through fifty-nine, and sixty-four or over, can contribute an additional $7,500 due to the catch-up provision. For those ages sixty to sixty-three, there's an additional catch-up contribution limit of $11,250.

It seems like there are a lot of limits on getting money into a Roth, and you may be thinking it's too late. No! It's never too late to kick Uncle Sam to the curb. Especially when tax rates are on sale.

I'm going to tell you a different strategy that has only one requirement—to have money in a tax-*deferred* investment. If you have money in the tax-deferred investment, you are allowed to move money from that bucket to the tax-free bucket. You do it via a strategy called a "Roth conversion." A true gift from Congress. Most of our clients are doing this right now. If you're not doing this now, or if you haven't done it over the last five to ten years, then you better start seeking help on this and explore it further.

# CHAPTER 9

# ROTH CONVERSIONS

Roth conversions are such an awesome opportunity, and one of my favorites. They're so popular right now that an article I wrote called "I Love Roth IRAs and Roth Conversions!" was featured on Kiplinger.com.[9] In the article, I emphasize the advantages of doing a Roth conversion.

There are two main reasons that now is a great time for a Roth conversion:

1. Taxes are currently "on sale."
2. Tax rates are likely going up.

Let's look at the details of turning a "forever-taxed" account into a "never-taxed-again" account.

## Conversion Basics

Why a Roth conversion makes sense can be understood by answering a question: Would you rather pay taxes on the

---

9    https://www.kiplinger.com/retirement/retirement-plans/
     roth-iras/604539/i-love-roth-iras-and-roth-conversions]

seed or the harvest? I'm from Carroll, Ohio, a rural farming community outside Columbus. One of my childhood friends is a farmer and has an apple orchard. I asked him, "Would you rather pay tax on the apple seeds you plant or on the harvest of those apples?" His answer was obvious: on the seed.

Roth conversions operate on a similar principle. For example, if you have $100,000, then you can pay taxes on that money now by doing a Roth conversion at a low tax rate, or you can wait until harvest and every dollar of growth during the intervening years would be taxable in an IRA.

Next, understand this: There are no limits for doing a Roth conversion. In other words, you can convert every IRA dollar you have, although we don't normally recommend doing so.

After hearing me speak at an event, a couple came to us at Peak Retirement Planning, Inc. with $3 million and a request to convert every dollar. I pulled out my calculator and calculated the total amount of tax they would have to pay. It was well over $1 million. We decided it was best to do a little at a time and do it over a specific number of years.

We do Roth conversions for people for as little as $1,000 to well above $1 million in one year. It depends on your situation. I call this type of strategy "filling the bucket" (see following picture). This is where you strategically convert enough so not to give you a heart attack but still convert enough so you don't end up in a higher tax bracket in the future. The key to deciding how much to convert involves assuming that your tax rate today will be lower than in the future. If that's the case, you want to convert. If you expect your total tax rate to be higher now than in the future, you wouldn't want to convert. Make sense? The goal is to pay the least amount of tax possible.

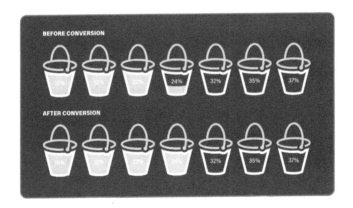

Why we didn't "allow" those clients to convert all at once is a matter of your total tax picture. You must worry about the effects of Social Security taxes, Medicare premiums, capital gains, net investment income, the five-year rule, deductions, and credits you may phase out of. Filling this bucket may not be as easy, fast, and clean as you may like. Don't get impatient—the right calculations will pay off in the long run in less tax. With our clients, we use advanced software to get us a more accurate picture.

Also keep in mind that the rules changed in 2017, where you can't modify a Roth conversion once initiated. We had someone share with us that she did a Roth conversion on her own for $11,000. However, when the paperwork got submitted and she looked it over, she saw that she had accidentally added an extra "1" and typed $111,000 for the Roth conversion amount instead of $11,000. That wasn't her plan at all. She tried to call the custodian where her money was to see if they would give her a break and correct the error, but they said, "The rules are the rules. Once a Roth conversion has been done, it can't be undone." Moral of the story: Make sure you're careful and seek help.

Distribution rules also prompt many clients to choose Roth conversions. Unlike a traditional IRA, with a Roth they don't have to take money out for required minimum distributions (RMDs). A traditional IRA requires you to pull out money starting in that year, but some people may not need that money at that time and would rather continue growing it tax-free for their beneficiaries, surviving spouse, emergencies, and more flexibility in the future.

## Tax Diversification

Tax diversification means not having all your eggs in one basket, so that's a big reason for finding ways to get more money into the tax-free bucket. If you have most of your money in one bucket, then you're probably not correctly allocated.

For example, if you have all your money in tax-deferred instruments, then you'll have no flexibility or control to fill the bucket or to be wise about keeping yourself in lower tax brackets in the future.

It could also be bad to have all your money in the tax-free bucket. Shocking? No. That means you would have already paid tax on everything and wouldn't have enough money to maximize the tax-free standard deduction in the future, nor have any money to give tax-free from an IRA to a charity.

Like many things in life, it's about balance. Just like you wouldn't want an investment portfolio that's in one single stock, you wouldn't want your investments to be taxed only one specific way. Again, not all your eggs in one basket.

## Tax Insurance for You

At Peak Retirement Planning, Inc. we like to think of the Roth IRA as "tax insurance." Since we think taxes will be higher, this allows us to not have to face the risks of paying higher taxes in the future.

Even if you think taxes could be lower, I would probably tell you to do a Roth anyway. Why? Tax diversification. I'm almost certain at some point during your lifetime you'll find yourself in a higher bracket, and if that's the case, you'll take from your Roth.

# CHAPTER 10

# BRACE YOURSELF— THERE IS A TAX BILL

I know, I know. You hate taxes.

If you do a Roth conversion, then you must pay tax on that money *today*. There is a tax bill, make no mistake.

Do we want to pay taxes right now? Yes.

Remember, taxes are on sale now. That's in your favor. But no sale lasts forever, so consider doing this right away. You either pay them now or later. Does this remind you of the Fram oil commercial from the 1970s?

## Pay Me Now or Pay Me Later:
### *The Fram Oil Commercial*

I love that old commercial. Some of you may recall it, where a mechanic shows the value of taking care of things now— before they become worse. He expresses the importance of buying a four-dollar Fram oil filter now and having no problems in the future, as opposed to not buying an oil filter now and having to pay two hundred dollars in the future to get it fixed.

He famously says, "The choice is yours. You can pay me now, or pay me later."

Uncle Sam is saying the same thing to you. You can pay your taxes now at a lower price during this tax sale period, or pay them later at a higher price. The choice is yours. Don't let Uncle Sam dictate your future. Take control so retirement doesn't have to be taxing.

## Best Way to Pay Taxes?

When it comes to paying taxes on Roth conversions, it's best to pay the taxes out of your pocket. If you have an extra amount in your bank account or if you have a taxable investment, then those are the places we look first. That way we can shift more money to the tax-free side.

For example, if you convert $100,000 and pay the taxes outside, then you now have $100,000 in your Roth. If you withhold the taxes from the investment, and if we assume a 25 percent tax rate withheld, then you would only be able to get $75,000 into the Roth.

However, if you don't have the money to pay out of your pocket right now, then it's usually still smart to withhold the taxes from the tax-deferred investment. Understand, if you're under age fifty-nine-and-a-half, then you can't withhold taxes from your tax-deferred investments unless you look at more advanced strategies. So be careful with conversions if you're under fifty-nine-and-a-half. If you're under fifty-nine-and-a-half and can pay the taxes out of pocket, then things will be easier for you.

## "I don't want to do a Roth conversion because I'll have less money."

We hear this frequently. And it's a big myth. People are confused about Roth conversions; even "financial experts" and other financial advisors get it wrong.

Here's a simple illustration to explain a Roth conversion:

If you have $100,000 in an IRA and convert it to a Roth (assuming a 25 percent tax rate) then you have $75,000. If you have $100,000 in an IRA and don't convert it to a Roth, then how much do you really have? Remember, you don't have $100,000 because of your partner, Uncle Sam. We can't assume the same tax rate applies, also leaving you $75,000. When you pay the tax, the rate might be double.

Let's say your investment doubles, and you end up with $150,000 in your Roth IRA and $200,000 in your IRA. Which would you rather have? They're technically the same value after you assume taxes come out, but in the Roth you have removed any future taxation. If tax rates in the future are, for example, 30 percent, then you save quite a bit of money.

To sum it up, if taxes remain the same, then worst case, you would end up with the same amount after taxes, assuming they're invested the same way. But I would still rather have the Roth IRA for the chance of not having higher tax rates along with all the other benefits of more control.

## Advantages of a Down Market

You've probably heard the advice about "When the market is down, don't make any changes; just wait for things to come back." I agree with that when it comes to *not* selling your investments when the market is down, but when it comes to tax planning, this isn't necessarily the best advice.

Some of the best opportunities when it comes to tax planning present themselves in a down market. For example, doing Roth conversions when the market is down is an excellent opportunity. It allows you to pay tax on a lower amount, get it into a Roth, and then get all the growth coming back tax-free.

Think of it like a Slinky toy. The market will go up and down over time, like the Slinky. When the Slinky is extended, the market is up; when the Slinky is coiled, the market is down. Would you rather pay taxes when the Slinky is stretched during the up market, or would you rather pay when the Slinky is coiled so that when the growth comes back it's all tax-free?

## Rule of 72

Another fun way to think about Roth conversions is when you think about the Rule of 72. The Rule of 72 says that your investment will double in twelve years if you get a 6 percent annual return.

For example, let's say you have $100,000 in your tax-deferred investment, if you take no action and let it sit there for twelve years. You'll then have $200,000. Great, right?

Yes. And no. Yes, it's great to see growth in your investments. No, it's not great to double your tax burden. If we assume a 25 percent rate, you could either pay taxes on the $100,000 today for $25,000, or pay it in twelve years on $200,000 for $50,000. Which would you rather do? Especially knowing that extra growth could continue to push you to higher brackets in the future and continue compounding.

### Rule of 72

$$72 \div \text{Annual Rate of Return} = \text{Time for Investment to Double}$$

$$72 \div 6\% = 12 \text{ Years}$$

**Rather pay taxes on $100,000 or $200,000?**

## In Summary: Roth Conversions

Roth IRAs sound like a miracle, don't they? Yet there are some reasons to convert and other reasons why you should not convert. Remember, everyone has different situations and there is no cookie-cutter financial plan. I've summarized some of the main reasons (there are others) for converting a Roth.

### Why You Should Do a Roth Conversion

1. Taxes are going up. By converting, you control when you pay taxes and the tax rate, and you maximize your lower brackets according to the rule of thumb "Defer when taxes are high, and pay when they are low."

2. You expect to be in a higher tax bracket in the future. Many people we work with will end up paying more in taxes due to pensions, Social Security, and required minimum distributions (RMDs).

3. To reduce your RMDs in the future.

4. To reduce your Medicare premiums in the future.

5. To reduce or eliminate Social Security tax in the future.

6. To reduce or eliminate capital gains tax in the future.

7. To allow for legacy planning. When your goal is to leave money to a spouse to lessen the widow's tax

or to leave money to your children, withdrawing a Roth is tax-free (remember, your dependents now must take out that amount over ten years, which could force them into higher tax brackets at unknown rates).

### Why You Should Not Do a Roth Conversion

1.  If you are sure to be in a lower (all-in) tax rate in the future (lower than today). The lower bracket might be due to high income now and low assets, retiring early, and having time to take advantage of lower brackets while you delay your Social Security benefit start date, pension, and before RMDs occur.

2.  If you need enough income from your tax-deferred investments to use the standard deduction we've discussed. So make sure you don't convert everything to leave that opportunity open to pay zero taxes.

3.  If your goal is to leave money behind to your children and they have a lower income than yours, or if you have multiple beneficiaries and each of them won't get a large amount (which won't bump them into a higher tax bracket).

4.  If you're charitably minded, since giving an IRA to a charity is tax-free with a qualified charitable

distribution (QCD) and at death (see chapter 16 for more information on this). We have a client with no children who is going to give all her money to charities, and in that case, she doesn't need a Roth.

5. If you're fairly certain you'll have high medical expenses in the future, and therefore could potentially have a large, itemized deduction year and significantly lower your income. (Alternatively, you can offset that loss with a strategy like a Roth conversion if you have more of a deduction than your income for that year.)

## Will the Roth IRA Go Away?

We get this question often. Personally, I don't think the Roth IRA will go away. However, as good planners, we must keep in mind that it could. Remember, the tax code is written in pencil, and Congress can change any part of it at any time.

When I look at the facts, I find it hard to believe that Congress would do away with the Roth IRA. There's so much more money in the tax-deferred bucket (over $30 trillion) in relation to the tax-free bucket (less than $1 trillion).

---

So where do you think the government would go to get their money? To the same place they go now: the tax-deferred buckets of Americans cashing in.

---

The other thing to understand is that it would not be politically wise for the government to tell all the people who have done an excellent job planning that the rules have severely changed against them. The government wants you to do a Roth right now with all the debt they're in. They need more revenue so they can keep spending more money.

But let's say the worst case happens and the Roth is changed. What would this look like? My guess is the changes wouldn't affect you too much or put you in a worse situation. Generally, Congress will phase things in and grandfather people in with these accounts so the hit isn't that bad.

What I could see Congress doing is making slight changes, like making required minimum distributions (RMDs) apply to Roth IRAs (right now they don't). They could prohibit new Roth contributions from being made.

Even under the worst-case situation, let's say Congress forces you to pay tax on the growth that has been tax-free over the years. That places you in a similar situation to the one you were in before.

Long story short, I wouldn't let this concern stop you from taking advantage of this great deal. Do everything you can with the rules you know to best position yourself. Not making changes is riskier than making changes.

## Roth and Tax Location Investing

Another pro tip for you if you have a Roth account is to seek growth in this investment. Why? All the growth is tax-free.

With our clients, we seek growth in any Roth accounts, but we're usually more conservative with the tax-deferred investments. The conservative investments may not grow as much, but they're more protected, so you have this trade-off, this balance, in your portfolio.

Our rule of thumb here: We must pay tax on the growth. So let's use the part of our plan where we aren't expecting as much growth.

The founder of PayPal, Peter Thiel, took this advice to the extreme. He understood how to be smart with tax planning and how to invest for growth in his Roth account. Peter Thiel started his Roth IRA with $2,000 and invested it into PayPal before it blossomed. With the growth of PayPal, his Roth IRA reached over $5 billion. And guess what? All that growth was tax-free. Smart man. (I bet he hates taxes too).

## The Five-Year Rule

The five-year rule is confusing to a lot of people.

Many people think, "I can't take money out of a Roth for five years after opening it." That can be true. But it doesn't apply to most of the people we work with. For most people, anything you contribute to a Roth IRA can be taken out at any time *without penalty or tax.*

We created a flow chart to understand how this rule could affect you. Follow the chart based on what you're doing and on your age.

The only time you run into issues with the five-year rule is if you do a conversion and are under age fifty-nine-and-a-half or haven't had a Roth open for five years.

The other area you could run into problems is on any earnings you receive from growth in your investment. If you're over age fifty-nine-and-a-half and have had a Roth for five years, then you're good to go. All other earnings would face a penalty or tax, or both, upon withdrawal.

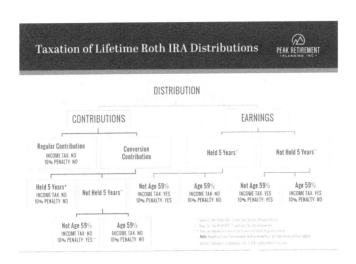

# CHAPTER 11

# LIKE WHAT YOU'RE HEARING?

Let's discuss some ways to get these strategies accomplished right now with your current retirement savings that you've spent all your years accumulating. This chapter is all about direct rollovers.

## Direct Rollover

A direct rollover is the term used when you're moving money from an employer-sponsored retirement plan (401(k), 403(b), TSP, etc.) to an IRA.

You might know from experience that you can roll your funds out of a 401(k) when you quit, are terminated, or retire from the job that provided you with the account. You will roll your funds directly into an IRA without making any withdrawals on the way.

When rolling money from any other tax-deferred investment, you want to make sure you're doing it correctly.

Getting any step wrong could have you paying penalties or taxes you didn't want—or need—to pay. Be ultracareful with this. We've seen people make mistakes on a rollover, and it can be costly.

You have to call your plan provider and ask them to do a direct rollover to your IRA. You may have to fill out paperwork to have it done. They'll either mail you a check or mail the money to a custodian who holds the money. If they mail you a check, you'll need to send that to the custodian where you want the money held so you don't have to pay taxes on it at that time. Your financial planner will guide you through this process and should take the steps for you.

We have a lot of clients who do rollovers so they can better plan for their financial retirement. The IRA has many more attractive investment options than a 401(k). A 401(k) may only have five to twenty options, whereas an IRA has many more. We've also seen people do rollovers for the opportunity to do Roth conversions since many 401(k) programs won't allow you to do in-plan Roth conversions.

## In-Service Rollover

What if you're still working but are over age fifty-nine-and-a-half? Well, then we have good news for you. Many of our clients implement a strategy called an "in-service rollover."

Since you can only do a direct rollover if you're retired or separated from the employer, the in-service rollover is a way you can still get a rollover done. Some plans allow you to do an in-service rollover to an IRA, which means you're allowed to do a rollover while you're still working, but only if you're over age fifty-nine-and-a-half. The other good news is that you'll still be able to contribute to your 401(k) or employer's retirement account to receive your free money from the company's match.

# CHAPTER 12

# BASICS OF REQUIRED MINIMUM DISTRIBUTIONS

One of the biggest nightmares for retirees with large tax-deferred investments as they grow older in retirement is the required minimum distribution, or RMD.

I get chills just thinking about it. Required minimum distributions are related to the mandated age, which is currently 73 (unless you were born in 1960 or after, in which case it is 75). When you reach that age, you're required to take a minimum amount out of your tax-deferred accounts. If you don't, you'll be penalized.

Not only are you required to take out money from your tax-deferred investments at that mandated age (and every year thereafter), but you must also pay taxes on the withdrawn (aka "distributed") amount that same year.

Uncle Sam knocks on your door and says, "You've gone years without paying taxes on your tax-deferred investments, and I'm in massive debt and need your money. Pay me now!"

In more technical terms, an RMD is a percentage, not a dollar amount. The percentage is based on the IRS life expectancy table. The older you get, the more that percentage increases. Uh-oh.

Most retirees not only see an increase in that percentage but also see their investments grow. This combination is deadly as it can cause issues when it comes to paying taxes. It could push you into a higher tax bracket and into a higher Medicare premium bracket, and it could cause Social Security to be more taxable and capital gains to be taxable or more taxable.

To illustrate how this works, see the following chart.

| RMD INPUTS | |
|---|---|
| Estimated Rate of Return | 6.00% |
| Account Balance | $1,000,000 |
| Owner Age | 73 |

| AGE | ACCOUNT BALANCE | RMD% | RMD |
|---|---|---|---|
| 73 | $1,000,000 | 3.78% | $37,800 |
| 74 | $1,019,932 | 3.93% | $40,083 |
| 75 | $1,038,640 | 4.07% | $42,273 |
| 76 | $1,056,149 | 4.22% | $44,569 |
| 77 | $1,072,274 | 4.37% | $46,858 |
| 78 | $1,086,941 | 4.55% | $49,456 |

| AGE | ACCOUNT BALANCE | RMD% | RMD |
|---|---|---|---|
| 79 | $1,099,734 | 4.74% | $52,127 |
| 80 | $1,110,463 | 4.96% | $55,079 |
| 81 | $1,118,707 | 5.16% | $57,725 |
| 82 | $1,124,641 | 5.41% | $60,843 |
| 83 | $1,127,626 | 5.65% | $63,711 |
| 84 | $1,127,750 | 5.96% | $67,214 |
| 85 | $1,124,168 | 6.25% | $70,260 |
| 86 | $1,117,142 | 6.58% | $73,508 |
| 87 | $1,106,252 | 6.95% | $76,885 |
| 88 | $1,091,130 | 7.30% | $79,652 |
| 89 | $1,072,166 | 7.76% | $83,200 |
| 90 | $1,048,304 | 8.20% | $85,961 |
| 91 | $1,020,083 | 8.70% | $88,747 |
| 92 | $987,216 | 9.26% | $91,416 |
| 93 | $949,548 | 9.91% | $94,100 |
| 94 | $906,775 | 10.53% | $95,483 |
| 95 | $859,969 | 11.24% | $96,660 |

You can see that the far right column, "RMD," goes up over time—that's because the "RMD percent" and the "account balance" grows. For illustrative purposes, we're assuming the account balance grows at a consistent 6 percent rate.

Let me walk through what happens at age seventy-three. You have $1 million and you multiply that by 3.78 percent (based on the life expectancy table) to give you $37,800 that you are required to take out. The chart shows how this can really add up over time. As you reach age ninety, you are now required to take out 8.2 percent of your investments, which in this example is just over the $1 million you started with, forcing you to take out $85,961. What will taking out that much money, plus Social Security, mean to your tax bracket? It will probably move much higher and at expected higher rates.

---

**Do you think RMDs are in your favor or Uncle Sam's?**

---

The good news is there are many strategies to take control and manage RMDs in a tax-wise manner.

# CHAPTER 13

# BASICS OF LEGACY PLANNING AND IRAs

If you plan to leave your IRA to your children or non-spouse, then you want to make sure you're aware of recent rule changes.

The non-spouse beneficiary used to be able to take the IRA funds over their lifetime, which wouldn't cause significant tax planning or tax issues. This was called a "stretch IRA." Now, they have to take the full amount of the IRA funds out within ten years.

If you have large tax-deferred investments, then you could see how this could lead to big issues in the future. If that's you, then you need to start planning for this, especially if your children are in a higher tax bracket than you. In that case, it would be wise to pay the tax now, while you can, as opposed to waiting and making your children do it at higher rates. You can either give more money to the government or to your children. The choice is yours.

We had a client who had a lot of wealth, and he wasn't fired up about his children getting his money. He wanted them to work hard for their money, as he had done all his life, and not rely on him. I get it. But here's the catch: He can't take his money with him when he dies. He ultimately decided that he hated paying taxes more than he hated giving money to his children. Fair enough.

A planning strategy you could do to lessen taxes is using the benefits of a Roth IRA. If you give the non-spouse a Roth IRA, then they still have to take it out in ten years, but it isn't taxed. They can also choose when to take it out over those ten years.

A strategy to be tax smart is to be aware of your children's tax situation. Leave the Roth IRAs to the higher-income children, and leave the IRAs that are taxed to the lower-income children. For example, we had clients where the son was a doctor and the daughter was a teacher. We gave the son the Roths and the daughter the IRAs so more money would end up passing to them free of tax.

If you have an inherited IRA (not Roth), waiting until the tenth year may not make sense. That may not be wise to do if tax rates are going up, and it all gets taxed at once. Unfortunately, that's what most people do before they see us. They don't understand the impact of their decision, so they stick to the status quo and don't do anything.

We typically advise people to take out the IRA now while the tax rates are on sale, or take it out little by little over time to avoid bumping up to the higher tax brackets.

You'll hear me say this a few times: *Doing nothing is worse*. Inaction in times of rapid change is the worst thing you can do. You must be proactive and smart, not reactive.

CHAPTER 14

# TWO VALUABLE TAX-FREE OPPORTUNITIES

As you've seen, Roth is the most popular tax-free planning strategy, but there are two other ideas you should definitely have on your radar depending on your situation. They are the health savings account (HSA) and life insurance.

## Health Savings Account

Health savings accounts, or HSAs, are one of my personal favorite investments. An HSA is a savings account that allows you to save and get tax benefits for qualified medical expenses. It offers what I call a trifecta—three tax advantages.

1. You get a tax deduction upfront, which saves you money today.
2. You get tax-deferred growth, which means you don't have to pay tax on the growth each year.

3. You get to use the funds tax-free for your health-care needs.

In my basketball days, I was a three-point shooter. For me, three was always better than two—and that's why this is one of my favorite investments.

I don't know about you, but I'm expecting all of us to have some kind of health-care needs in the future. We recommend people to have their HSA maxed out after they do the company match in their 401(k).

---

**The trifecta effect makes the HSA
better than a Roth IRA.**

---

We also recommend, like the Roth, to invest in the HSA for growth and wait as long as possible to use it to maximize the tax-free growth component, or use it when tax rates are higher.

I see people who use their HSA for health expenses today, but we suggest they pay those immediate expenses out of pocket if they can. If you're worried you won't need health care in the future (you may want to wake up if you believe that), or if you want to be a better planner and save money on taxes, then save your receipts and you'll get them reimbursed at any time through your HSA. This is noted in the IRS notice 2004-50. As long as you've had an HSA set up before the health-care receipt date, you can do this.

For example, maybe tax rates are 50 percent, and you have a pile of receipts to write off. This might be a good year to submit them all and save 50 percent. Or maybe the market is down, and if your HSA is invested for growth, it will probably be down as well. That would *not* be the best time to take out from the HSA. Instead, pay out of pocket, save your receipts, and when the market comes back up, submit your receipts for reimbursement to avoid taking out money when the market is down.

The HSA is a great strategy, and we're happy the IRS allows it. You just have to know the rules and know how to work around them and within them.

This opportunity isn't for everyone, however. You can't benefit from an HSA if you're on Medicare or if you don't have a high-deductible health insurance plan that allows an HSA contribution.

## Advanced Strategy: The Beauty of Life Insurance

Life insurance is, among other labels we give to it, a tool in the toolbox.

Most people think of life insurance as a way to seek protection for family members in the case of your sudden death when they're still counting on you to pay the bills.

But life insurance becomes a strategic vehicle when seeking tax benefits—especially the more you've saved.

And that's why you would get life insurance—not only to make sure your family is taken care of but also to make sure Uncle Sam *isn't* taken care of.

In other words, a life insurance policy—the right one—could provide tax benefits.

Here are some benefits and explanations of why and where life insurance makes sense.

### *Tax-Free Death Benefit*

If you're looking to leave a legacy to friends or family members, you should consider life insurance.

I like to compare the advantages of life insurance to coins. Imagine putting one coin into the life insurance policy. When you pass away, the policy will spit out three coins. What's more, no tax is due on those three coins.

If you're near estate tax limits (or expect to be in the future), then life insurance could be another attractive place to put your money. You would want to look at using an irrevocable life insurance trust for this type of planning. That way, your heirs won't be left paying a flat 40 percent tax on your money. This is a more advanced strategy for those who are considered "high net worth." For most, reaching estate tax limits may not be a concern right now, with the estate tax at $13.99 million per individual in 2025, but I would expect this to be much lower in the future (as it's been less than $1 million in the past).

### Tax-Free If You Need Long-Term Care

Many life insurance companies will offer various "riders." These are ways to modify the standard policy for some type of additional coverage.

You can add a rider for long-term care coverage. This allows you to accelerate your death benefit tax-free and use it for long-term care benefits if needed. Some carriers offer a no-cost rider called an "accelerated benefits rider." You'll want to make sure your policy allows riders for the specific purpose you have in mind as not every company offers such an opportunity.

The high cost of long-term care has become a big concern for many. Riders can be an especially effective way to plan for long-term care, as long-term care insurance has become so costly. With a rider, you also don't have to worry about "use it or lose it."

The statistics are not in our favor. Over 70 percent of retirees will need long-term care after age sixty-five. The costs of long-term care could be significant, anywhere between $50,000 to $100,000 a year, depending on the care you receive and the state you live in (a high- or low-cost-of-living state).[10]

---

10   https://www.genworth.com/aging-and-you/finances/cost-of-care.html.

Many of you have probably had a family member who needed long-term care. I've seen family members go through it, and it's stressful emotionally and financially. I urge you to plan for it in one way or another.

### Tax-Free Income

Life insurance as a tax-free income strategy isn't for everyone. At our firm we only consider this for people who don't have any other options for saving money in tax-free ways.

This strategy could work for someone who maxes out their Roth IRA, maxes out their Roth 401(k), maxes out their HSA option, has an adequate amount in their taxable bucket (we'll discuss this soon), and maxes out their Roth conversion opportunities each year.

## Life Insurance in Summary

You must be careful with life insurance. It's incredibly complex, and studying and choosing the right policy from the right carrier calls for a lot of meticulous work. Life insurance isn't a DIY strategy. There are flaws to this tool. You want to work with an expert.

---

**Remember, there's no perfect place for your money.**

---

Life insurance can be a good planning tool for diversification purposes. Life insurance has different rules and no limits, unlike other investments.

We don't know the future of taxes, nor do we know what the market will do. Life insurance gives you the opportunity to put your money in another place under different rules so that your eggs aren't all in one basket.

Note that I would never recommend that someone put all their money in life insurance, but a portion could make sense for the right person. I have a permanent life insurance policy to achieve tax savings; so do many celebrities and CEOs. You can even find an article online about University of Michigan football former coach Jim Harbaugh who was offered a substantial life insurance policy as an added benefit for coaching at the school.

You may also hear of life insurance as the "rich man's Roth IRA." It's worth looking into if you have a higher income or higher net worth.

Still, you want to be careful with life insurance; it isn't a good fit for everyone. You need to watch out for your standard insurance salesperson who's only looking to get a commission check rather than understand your entire financial plan and how it works within everything else you have going on. Instead, consult a comprehensive financial planner who knows insurance.

# CHAPTER 15

# BASICS OF THE TAXABLE BUCKET

Let's discuss investments that you have in the taxable bucket, where you're only taxed on gains. Some of these taxable-bucket investments have labels such as non-qualified, individual, or joint, or they could be labeled in a trust's name. Real estate and businesses would be held in this category. These investments are taxed at the prevailing capital gains rates.

Most people think the only capital gains rate is 15 percent. That's correct for most people, but you could also be in a 0 percent or a 20 percent bracket for long-term capital gains.

There has been talk of capital gains changing to ordinary income entirely or for higher-income people (another instance of legislative risk). This hasn't happened, but it's something to keep an eye on. Keep in mind, short-term capital gains—gains that have happened within a year—are taxed as ordinary income. To avoid this, we would recommend you wait at least a year to sell off an investment in this bucket.

| LONG-TERM CAPITAL GAINS (2025) | | |
|---|---|---|
| Tax Rate | Single | Married Filing Jointly |
| 0% | $0 | $0 |
| 15% | $48,350 | $96,700 |
| 20% | $533,400 | $600,050 |

The preceding chart shows long-term capital gains rates.

Again, with the taxable investment bucket, you're only taxed on gains.

This bucket primarily holds your non-retirement investment accounts. Say you threw $10,000 into an E*TRADE trading account ten years ago. This is a taxable investment account. You may recall that every time you filed taxes, your accountant asked you for that trading account statement. This statement showed your gains on that $10,000 account over the tax year, and that's taxable gain.

That $10,000 doesn't sound like a lot to worry about, does it? Well, loads of our clients have several *hundred* thousand dollars in such accounts, which can cause big issues if not addressed the right way.

For example, say that $10,000 account grows to $12,000, and you decide to sell it after one year. You'll pay capital gains on only the $2,000 "profit" at capital gains rates. Let's say you're in the 15 percent bracket. In this case, you'll pay $300 to Uncle Sam, and you'll end up with $11,700. The $10,000 isn't taxed since you've already paid taxes on that portion. How? You took some of your past *taxed* income and opened the E*TRADE account with that.

---

**The government is being nice here and not making you pay double taxes.**

---

Also, don't forget about net investment income if your income exceeds $200,000 as a single filer or $250,000 as a married filing jointly filer. Then you could pay an additional 3.8 percent tax on all investment income.

## What Is Cost Basis?

It's important to know your cost basis with these tax bucket investments. Your cost basis is the amount of money you've already paid taxes on. The $10,000 you initially put in your

E*TRADE account had already been subject to taxes, in other words.

The place where your investment is held may not have this cost basis fully calculated for you. That means you need to go back and calculate it yourself or get help from a CPA. Brokerages weren't required to keep the cost basis until 2008, so potentially you would have to calculate what it was before then.

If you don't have a cost basis, then all your money will be taxed at the capital gains rate—so get help figuring it out.

Many people like this taxable bucket for one reason: Your money is liquid, and you can take it out without penalties (unlike retirement accounts, but more on those later). There's also no limit to how much you can fund them with (again, unlike retirement accounts).

## Rental Property Income

Rental properties are where we see people pay the most in capital gains tax.

My dad has a lot of rental properties, so this is something we regularly revisit and plan with him. His process will be familiar to you: He buys the properties at a low price, fixes them up, keeps them for long enough to see an appreciation in the value, has tenants paying rent from the beginning, then sells them when he has a gain he's happy with.

With my dad being retired, he doesn't want as many headaches with the properties, so we've been selling them off during the recent seller's market. This leads to a lot of work and tax planning, but it's worth every second.

## Primary Residence

For your primary residence, you may be exempt from capital gains. If you sell your house and the gain is less than $250,000 (filing single) or $500,000 (filing married), then you pay no taxes.

There are many other things you'll want to understand about selling your primary residence, and you may want to look at this strategy closer if you have rental properties. You could sell your primary residence under these rules and then go live in one of your rentals that has a lot of appreciated gain. You would have to live there for two out of the last five years and make it your primary residence; you could avoid taxes if you met all the other requirements. This is something I'm currently doing.

## Your Business Interests

The other way we see people use tax planning with this taxable bucket is when selling businesses. We see people who have owned businesses for thirty or more years. If this is you, consider a few strategies such as installment sales, donor-advised funds (DAFs), and charitable remainder trusts (CRTs). Those are some of the popular strategies we have used with clients. Make sure to get help on something this advanced, especially if you've seen lots of growth in your business over the years.

## How to Get to the 0 Percent Capital Gains Bracket

As I mentioned, most people are in the 15 percent capital gains bracket. But why not be in the 0 percent bracket? You can be, by doing smart, timely planning to lower your income in the future.

---

**With timely and smart planning, many of our clients "live" in the 0 percent bracket. Their capital gains are tax-free.**

---

Let's look at a few real-world examples of the consequences of not doing timely, smart tax planning.

### Soaring Stock Values

I want to share an example of one of our clients who owned Apple stock. His cost basis was $20,000 (the amount he paid taxes on and funded his Apple stock with). The value of his Apple stock went all the way up to $120,000. Quite a gain in any market, right? It meant a big tax bill if he wasn't smart about it.

But good for him—he's working with us, and we know the rules. He retired at the end of 2022. He has one particular year that he can sell his stock; if sold that year, he'll pay no tax on the gain. Wow. But if he sells it in any other year, he'll have to pay tax.

During this client's working years, he was over the 0 percent bracket limit, so he would have to pay 15 percent tax if he sold his Apple stock. But also in his retirement years, his Social Security, pension, and investment withdrawals will push him over the 0 percent bracket. So how does he get this Apple stock sold and pay no tax? By understanding how everything works together, that's how. By delaying his Social Security benefit start date, his pension start date, and by not taking any money from his other investments in the year after he retires, it's possible to pay no tax on the gain.

Our client did this, and his income for 2023 was going to be $0. He then sold the $100,000 gain of his Apple stock— and *still* kept his taxable income in the 0 percent bracket. This is due to the amount of his standard deduction, plus almost $90,000, which gives him more room than he needs to sell it off at no tax. Not only that, but we also had room left in 2023 to do a Roth conversion at a 0 percent tax rate while still keeping the capital gains at 0 percent!

To put this strategy in perspective, our firm has many other clients who are in their late fifties and sixties and have taken early retirement and haven't collected Social Security. To give them the income they need, we could go to their highly appreciated taxable investments that have been accumulating for many years and sell them off—while keeping them in the 0 percent tax bracket.

## Stepped-Up Basis Costs

Another thing to understand with taxable investments is the step-up in basis. Current rules state that if you pass away, your taxable investments will get a step-up in basis when left to a beneficiary—a reason phantom gains (discussed next) can come around to haunt you.

We were working with a client who didn't have much longer to live. Their former advisor recommended she sell off the funds in her taxable investment account, which had highly appreciated, to invest in something else. If she did that, she would have to pay a large amount of capital gains tax. She had no need for the money, and her biggest goal was leaving money to her children. Instead, we advised her to not sell the funds and hold on to them. When she passed away a few years later, the step-up meant no tax was due. Her children happily received more money, and Uncle Sam inherited nothing. What more could she have wanted?

This same stepped-up basis concept applies to other taxable investments we've discussed. Keep that in mind.

## More Advanced: Phantom Gains, Tax Aware, Cost Aware

The other thing I want you to be aware of with the taxable investment is "phantom gains." Phantom gains are the gains that you must pay on mutual funds every year.

Phantom gains occur because mutual funds aren't "tax aware." They sell off holdings from the fund throughout the year without considering the tax impact since their only focus is trying to maximize returns. That's why you pay more for the active management in a mutual fund. Active management can be good, but not usually in your taxable investment.

I always tell people you shouldn't invest your non-qualified (taxable) investments the same as you invest your qualified (tax-deferred or tax-free) investments, because they're taxed differently.

In a qualified account, it doesn't matter, from a tax standpoint, when things are bought and sold—as long as the money isn't withdrawn from the account. In this instance, active management is okay to do in this account, and we typically recommend it be that way for our clients. This allows people to take advantage of market trends when they present themselves.

One downside is that if you have active management with a mutual fund in your taxable investment, you won't get to choose when to pay the taxes. You'll be forced to pay taxes whenever the mutual fund manager wants to, and they'll almost never have your specific situation in mind.

On a side note, you need to be "cost aware" if you own a mutual fund, especially if you're paying a financial advisor to invest in mutual funds. You could be paying two fees, an advisor's fee and the internal expenses of the mutual fund, which can really add up. Part of the advisor's fee could be a commission upfront, which doesn't encourage them to give you the service you deserve. Plus, many bigger firms have revenue agreements with mutual fund companies to offer mutual funds to their clients. Doing so gives the firms more pay. You can find this disclosure on a firm's website— revenue agreements present a conflict of interest, and the firm must disclose it. If you're working with a bigger company, you may notice the majority of your holdings are with the same company. I wonder why.

If your advisor isn't doing comprehensive planning, then you could really be overpaying for the service you're getting. Professional investment management can be received at a much lower cost. I'm not saying mutual funds are bad investments. There's just a lot to be aware of when investing in them.

We typically recommend clients manage their taxable investments through a passive approach, meaning don't buy and sell continually. Instead, buy and sell when the opportunity presents itself. We prefer to do this through either individual stocks or exchange-traded funds (ETFs). These investments may pay out dividends throughout the year on which you'll have to pay tax, but you'll likely have much less tax since there isn't consistent trading. This gives you the chance to sell the funds in opportunistic years, like gifting the highly appreciated assets to a charity or to a donor-advised fund to avoid taxes on the gain. Or you can use the o percent bracket in the future that we discussed earlier.

For example, as part of my personal portfolio, I bought seven stocks from reputable companies that had fallen during market turbulence that I hope will go up over time. If I'm right, and they do grow (so far they have), then over time I will have massive gains in these stocks. I never plan to touch these stocks (no buying or selling). Instead, I see these as my "giving stocks." I'll gift them to the charities that are dear to my heart and pay no tax on them. That action will allow me to gift more to charity and gift less to Uncle Sam.

## More Advanced: Capital Gains versus Ordinary Income

For those more advanced, if you have a lot of money in bank accounts, money markets, CDs, treasuries, and annuities, consider changing them from the "ordinary income" tax they are currently under to investments taxed as capital gains. If you hold money in these buckets, then these can also be considered in the "taxable bucket," but understand these accounts are not at the favorable capital gain rates we just discussed. They would be under ordinary income taxes, as we discussed earlier in the book.

In other words, instead of paying zero capital gains on growth, you could pay 12 percent on that gain. Instead of paying 15 percent capital gains, you could be paying 22 or 24 percent on that gain. Instead of paying 20 percent capital gains, you could be paying 37 percent on that gain. Do you see where your hard-earned money will be headed if you don't act?

So how do we do smart tax planning here? We normally suggest you invest this money in investments that incorporate capital gains like stocks and index funds. Then, if you still like the idea of having the safe investments (bank accounts, money markets, CDs, treasuries, annuities), hold those in your IRA. You can still have the level of protection with your investments, but you'll "reposition" your assets to be more tax smart.

Changing your investments from being taxed as ordinary income to being taxed as capital gains is a strong strategy because those vehicles I mentioned that are taxed as ordinary income could be taxed throughout the year. This means you have no control over how much taxable interest you'll have, which will force your taxable income higher. By moving your money to a capital gains investment, we can have more control when we want to initiate a taxable event.

Let us take the "repositioning" idea even further and bring back our friend Roth that we discussed earlier. We often recommend people who have a large amount in their bank accounts or in taxable investments to max out their Roth 401(k) and Roth IRAs if they're not doing so already. That way they can get more money in the tax-free bucket and get that money growing tax-free. Instead of paying ordinary income tax or capital gains tax on the growth, put it in a Roth where you pay no tax on the growth!

Let's use an example. Suppose we had $100K invested and it doubled to $200K. How much would we pay, depending on the investment account it was in?

- Capital Gains (assuming 15 percent capital gains bracket): $15K taxes
- Ordinary Income (assuming 22% tax bracket): $22K
- Roth: $0

## More Advanced: Real Estate

Many tax benefits come with real estate. A real estate investment could be categorized in the taxable bucket or in the tax-free bucket.

As you know, many of the nation's wealthy own real estate in some way—but you don't have to for wealth building. Most people understand that real estate comes with headaches and a lot of work, so this investment isn't for everybody. We have clients who prefer not to have real estate beyond their personal residence, even though they understand the value such an asset can bring to a retirement plan. They prefer to keep their financial life simpler, which definitely makes sense.

If you're like them, or you already have enough money to fund your retirement, maybe you don't need complex and advanced real estate strategies to get to the finish line and accomplish your retirement goals. Plus, some people simply don't have goals of building the biggest barns. They want manageable financials that can grow consistently over time with less risk and less work.

For those of you who hold real estate or are interested in learning more about the advantages of doing so, let's keep going.

When you sell investment real estate—that is, a property that is not your primary residence—you have to pay capital gains as mentioned. There are some ways, however, to avoid these capital gains and make real estate tax-free. Real estate could arguably be in the tax-free bucket because, depending on how you use the strategies attached to it, you could have no taxes on your real estate over a number of years and get many tax savings each year.

### Depreciation

If you're in the game of real estate for the long haul, then one tax benefit for you is depreciation. Depreciating the property means you get tax write-offs each year. You can depreciate real estate year after year over a significant period of time—often thirty to forty years—depending on the use of the building. But can you speed this up?

### Cost Segregation

I'll give you some advice that I personally use with real estate. If you own real estate as an investment, you may not want to own that real estate for longer than seven years or so. If you use the cost segregation strategy, you can write off parts of the building over a shorter period of time (for example, five to seven years). Thus you don't have to wait the full thirty to forty years to get your depreciation. Basically, you can get a portion of your depreciation in a shorter amount of time.

Some of you are ahead of me and might say, "When we eventually sell the real estate, we'll have to recapture that depreciation and pay taxes on it. So you're having us write it off now to pay it back later. How does that get us ahead financially? Tell us why this is a useful strategy?"

### The IRS Section 1031 Advantage

The IRS Tax Code Section 1031 "like-kind exchange" allows you to exchange one property for another, and this is considered a tax-free exchange. No taxes would be paid, and now you would do the "cost segregation" again on this building over the next five to seven years. When the time comes, you repeat with a new 1031 like-kind exchange and also repeat the cost segregation.

Over time, this is a powerful strategy. Let's say you bought a property for $1 million. If you decide to do cost segregation over the next seven years, maybe you could depreciate 25 percent of the building by that time. That means you would be able to write off $250,000 of income from your taxes. If you're in an approximate 30 percent total tax bracket, as an example, you just saved $75,000 in taxes.

Then let's say you do a 1031 exchange, and at the time of exchange, your property is worth $1.5 million. You exchange for another property worth $1.5 million. No tax is assessed if you do it the right way with professional assistance. You then do cost segregation again on this property, and 25 percent of $1.5 million allows you to write off $375,000, which could be another $112,500 of tax savings, assuming a 30 percent tax bracket. So you have $187,500 in your pocket.

Then let's say you pass away after buying this property and leave it to your children. Your children now receive the $1.5 million property without paying any taxes, due to the stepped-up cost basis that we discussed.

That's how you can have real estate be part of your tax-free bucket now while you are living and also when you pass away. If you've heard of the advantages of real estate and how the wealthy have taken advantage of it, this is one of many ways that they do it.

It's important to know that any and all tax rules can change—have I mentioned how our tax code is written in pencil?—and there's a lot more that goes into this. This is just a high-level overview of the value of real estate if you want to do something extra to build your tax-free bucket.

Many of our clients may not need to do this, but they might do it for fun. I use these strategies myself.

# CHAPTER 16

# CHARITABLE STRATEGIES

If your goal is to give to charities, make sure you receive your tax benefits. A lot of tax benefits are associated with charitable giving, so let's make you aware of some of my favorites.

## Qualified Charitable Distribution

If you are charitably minded, then the qualified charitable distribution (QCD) is a wonderful opportunity to take advantage of once you're age seventy-and-a-half or older. A QCD is when you can start giving money from your IRA to a charity—tax-free.

We had a client who was giving $10,000 a year to his church out of his pocket. We told him if he gave that money from his IRA, then he would pay no taxes on that distribution. We ran the numbers and showed him he would save over 25 percent in taxes. He was in the 22 percent federal tax bracket and ended up paying about 3 percent in state tax. Saving $2,500 sure made him happy.

A simple change in the account he was giving from made these kinds of savings possible, and he was smart enough to understand that the tax rules are there to take full, legal advantage of. He didn't give more or less than he was giving to charities before, but the tax advantage provided him with more money in his pocket.

Another neat opportunity with QCDs is that once you reach required minimum distribution age, you can start having this charitable giving count toward your RMD. For example, if your RMD requires you to take out $20,000 a year from your IRA, and you give $5,000 to a charity, you're only required to now take out $15,000, and that's counted toward income. The $5,000 is exempt from income tax. A great deal for you! And not Uncle Sam. Which is what we like, right?

## Donor-Advised Fund

The donor-advised fund (DAF) is fun to use when tax planning. If you're charitably minded, DAFs are a terrific way to give more efficiently and pay less tax in the process.

A DAF really isn't a fund but an account managed by a sponsoring organization. You can deposit assets for donation to charity over time in the DAF account. You're the one who recommends how to invest the assets, and you still get to decide where to donate your money. You, the donor, get a tax deduction for making contributions into the DAF in the year you make the contribution, allowing a unique tax-planning opportunity for that particular year.

Donor-advised funds are a way you can get over that standard deduction hump in one year and then give from your DAFs ongoing and use the same standard deduction you would have used without leaving deductions on the table to not be used. This is an especially great strategy for people who have highly appreciated assets in their taxable bucket. It allows them to not have to pay tax on that growth and allows them to get a tax deduction upfront. They can itemize instead of taking the standard deduction as just mentioned.

I want to bring back our client with the Apple stock to this example to show you another tax-planning opportunity he had. He could gift his $120,000 stock to a DAF and pay zero tax on it. On top of that, he would get an itemized deduction this year of $120,000. Isn't that much better than the $30,000 standard deduction?

This client gives about $10,000 a year, so what we would do is not give this money to the charities out of his pocket for the next twelve years. Instead, we would give the money from his DAF, and his charitable goal is accomplished, along with over $15,000 in tax savings from not paying capital gains. That's an additional year and a half of giving for him. (Or he could buy a boat). The good news is that the choice is yours when giving and saving that much money. Plus, let's not forget that this client saved over $25,000 by itemizing rather than taking the standard deduction as well.

For example, if our client gave $10,000 each year, he wouldn't exceed the $30,000 standard deduction. That means his charitable gift was a waste, from a tax-planning standpoint. His total deduction over the ten years (assuming $30,000 standard deduction each year, for easy numbers) is $300,000. For him, the DAF makes his deductions more beneficial because it allows him to itemize his deductions for one year with $120,000 worth of deductions. This would mean he would technically have $0 of charitable deductions ongoing but could now take the standard deduction. That puts total deductions over the ten years at $390,000 ($120,000 year one + $30,000 for the next nine years).

---

**Would you rather have $390,000
of deductions or $300,000? Hard decision.**

---

There are more ways to leverage a DAF and save a boatload of money in taxes. You just have to know the rules and opportunities.

For our clients under age seventy-and-a-half, we use this strategy to give them enough to give from the DAF until they reach age seventy-and-a-half. Once they do, we give from their IRAs to their charities (aka a QCD as mentioned previously) since, in our thinking, that strategy could equate to more of a tax saving at that time if tax rates go up.

## Charitable Remainder Trust

The charitable remainder trust (CRT) strategy has you giving money now to a CRT to get the tax benefits today. By giving to a CRT, you get to enjoy an income stream from the trust for the rest of your life while still receiving the tax benefits upfront. When you die, the "remainder" of the money goes to charity—again giving you all the tax benefits since it's a charitable deduction.

The CRT is more of an advanced strategy, but we've seen it used with success, even for those without charitable goals. Think about it—if you live a long time, there won't be as much to leave behind to charities.

We see this strategy used mostly for people selling highly appreciated assets to lessen capital gains tax, like selling a business, real estate, or highly appreciated stocks or assets.

## For My Neighbors in Ohio

If you're passionate about giving to Christian causes and live in Ohio, then you'll be interested in one of my favorite tax-planning strategies, the Ohio Christian Education

Network Scholarship Granting Organization (OCEN SGO). I can't stop telling people about it. Like I've said before, I don't agree with everything the government spends my money on, but the OCEN SGO allows me to use the tax money I'm required to pay and have it go to a Christian organization, something aligned with my values that I agree with.

### Ohio Christian Education Network Scholarship Granting Organization

Do you like donating money and seeing the impact of it? How about donating money to benefit children in our community when it costs you *nothing*.

With the OCEN SGO, you can donate $750 per year ($1,500 per year if you are married and each spouse makes a separate $750 donation) to benefit children at Christian schools. You will then receive a $750 dollar-for-dollar tax credit to reduce your state taxes per spouse. This means you receive every dollar back that you donated. For example, if your state tax due is $878.42, a $750 donation would reduce your state tax to $128.42.

Too good to be true? Exactly my thoughts when I first heard of this opportunity. After further research, I realized it is true and how impactful this can be for not only you but also families who are seeking an affordable Christian education for their children. You can choose which school (kindergarten through twelfth grade) your donation goes to, and you may even be able to have the donation go toward a specific student if they qualify. To learn more about OCEN SGO, find a list of schools available for donation, or make a donation, go to Ohiocen.org.

Regarding your tax credit, the OCEN SGO deduction is more impactful than the usual charitable deduction that only reduces your taxable income. The credit you receive is a reduction in the amount of tax you owe; therefore, the amount you give is the amount you get back (up to $750 each). Also, if you're age seventy-and-a-half or older, you can donate money from your IRA directly to a charity, tax-free (the QCD). This means you can give money from your IRA to receive this benefit and also get the state tax credit.

# CHAPTER 17

# STATE TAXES

This chapter will provide a brief overview of the type of state taxes you need to be aware of. We have clients across the country, so this is something with which we're familiar. We know how to maximize planning for state taxes.

Many people flock to Florida, Tennessee, or Texas to take advantage of zero state income tax. That's fine. What you need to understand, though, is that you shouldn't make this decision strictly because of income tax.

There are a variety of state taxes that form a holistic picture of what taxes could look like in any given state. For example, you could be paying higher property tax or a higher sales tax in exchange for zero income taxes. Every state must get their money somehow.

I hope this chapter will offer you guidance and considerations when deciding if you should move to a different state in retirement.

Top Marginal State Individual Income Tax Rates (as of January 3, 2023)

Source: "State Individual Income Tax Rates and Brackets for 2023," Timothy Vermeer, February 21, 2023, https://taxfoundation.org/state-income-tax-rates-2023/.

## Property Tax

There are two important considerations when choosing to move to another state: the property tax rate for that state and the cost of real estate in that state. States with higher real estate values will naturally result in more property taxes, even if they have lower tax rates. In some cases, it may not be more tax conscious to move to a state with lower property tax rates, based solely on real estate value.

For example, Hawaii has the lowest property tax rate at 0.27 percent, but it also has the highest median home value among all states.[11] It's not all about the rates. When

_____

11    https://smartasset.com/taxes/hawaii-property-tax-calculator.

considering the complete tax picture, a state like Texas may not be the best option for your needs. Although they have no income taxes, you'll see one of the highest property tax rates in the Lone Star State. You could compare that to South Carolina, on the other hand, where you would pay both income and property taxes but at a lower overall tax rate.

## Sales Tax

Will you spend a significant amount on discretionary items? Forty-five out of fifty states will have sales tax, varying from 1.76 percent to 9.55 percent when combining state and local sales tax rates. The more of your income that you'll spend on sales-taxed items will determine how big of an impact sales tax will have on your overall state tax burden.

**How High are Sales Taxes in Your State?**
*Combined State & Average Local Sales Tax Rates, January 2023*

Source: State and Local Sales Tax Rates," Janelle Fritts, February 7, 2023, https://taxfoundation.org/2023-sales-taxes/.

## Estate Tax and Inheritance Tax

When deciding to move states, consider the estate tax rates and the inheritance tax. Estate tax rates can be as high as 20 percent. The inheritance tax is a tax levied directly upon your beneficiaries, and it's based upon the state in which they live. Only six states charge an inheritance tax. If you have a large estate and goals for your legacy, you'll need to understand how your state will tax your wealth when you're gone.

To clarify, we're not discussing federal estate taxes, which in 2025 only apply to those with over $13.99 million. Federal estate taxes will be levied directly on the value of your estate, reducing the amount your heirs will receive.

While the federal estate tax exemption currently applies to only a small number of Americans, there are twelve states that will levy an additional estate tax, with exemptions as low as $1 million in states like Oregon and Massachusetts. There are many more people in these states who will see their wealth taxed after they're gone, even if they don't cross the federal exemption.

## Retirement Income (IRA/401(k)/Pensions)

For retirees drawing income from their IRAs, 401(k)s, or pensions, understanding the state income tax is just the beginning.

Some states like Illinois, Texas, and Tennessee, among others, don't tax retirement income taken from retirement accounts. If you took $100,000 in income from your 401(k) here in Ohio, you're going to pay around $4,000 in state taxes. In Illinois, however, you could withdraw $100,000 from your 401(k) and pay zero taxes (even though they have a state income tax rate of 4.95 percent).

The type of income you plan to receive is going to be a major factor in which states will provide the most tax advantages for you. If you have a large amount in tax-deferred investments, where you live could play a key role in how much you either spend or save in taxes.

## Social Security Tax

**Does Your State Tax Social Security Benefits?**
*State Tax Treatment of Social Security Benefits, 2021*

Source: "How Does Your State Treat Social Security Income?" Janelle Fritts, May 26, 2021, https://taxfoundation.org/states-that-tax-social-security-benefits-2021/.

Thirteen states tax Social Security benefits at some level, and even among these states, there are many differences on how they're taxed. Here in Ohio, we pay no taxes on Social Security benefits at the state level. In Vermont, Social Security would be taxed at the state level if a married couple reported $44,000 or more in adjusted gross income.

In sum, before you pack up to move to states like Tennessee or Florida to live a life of no state income tax, take inventory of your specific situation and how the other revenue generators for the state will come into play. Consider your spending habits, income sources, legacy goals, and even the value of your home to understand the holistic tax picture and identify the unique opportunities that may be available to you.

# CHAPTER 18

# MEDICARE PREMIUM BASICS

When doing tax planning, you must also keep Medicare premiums in mind and understand how they work. The amount you pay for Medicare premiums is based on your income. The higher your income, the more you pay for Medicare premiums—even though you don't get any extra benefits.

To my point earlier in the book, the government penalizes savers and people who have been smart with their money. You will pay more than someone who didn't save. I don't know about you, but I don't like that incentive. It's not an effective way to motivate and reward hard work and doing the right thing.

Like Social Security, Medicare is in trouble. The cost of Medicare has increased over the years to count for the increased need of health care. The baby boomer generation is rolling through and in high demand of health care. Who will pay for this care?

This isn't for certain going to happen, but I expect Medicare to continue to increase in cost and maybe even lower the tiers of how much people pay in premiums. This means the government could lower the current $212,000 first tier that increases your premium if you are married filing jointly (see following chart). My point? Keep your income *lower* in the future to have more control and limit Uncle Sam's ability to get more of your money.

| MEDICARE PREMIUMS | | |
|---|---|---|
| If your yearly income in 2023 was: | | You pay each month (in 2025) |
| File individual tax return | File joint tax return | |
| $106,000 or less | $212,000 or less | $185.00 |
| above $106,000 up to $133,000 | above $212,000 up to $266,000 | $259.00 |
| above $133,000 up to $167,000 | above $266,000 up to $334,000 | $370.00 |
| above $167,000 up to $200,000 | above $334,000 up to $400,000 | $480.90 |
| above $200,000 and less than $500,000 | above $400,000 and less than $750,000 | $591.90 |
| $500,000 or above | $750,000 or above | $628.90 |

Living a tax-free retirement, or close to it, keeps you off Uncle Sam's radar.

## Medicare Premium Calculation

Medicare starts at age sixty-five. But the way they calculate the amount you pay is based on your income two years prior. *That's not a typo.* Like in my chart, the premium you pay for 2025 will be based on what your income was in 2023.

To further clarify, your income in 2024 will determine your 2026 Medicare premium. You won't see this until two years later. We see people all the time who don't understand how this works and are frustrated when there's more coming out of their Social Security benefits two years after having a high-income year.

One client of ours couldn't fathom why his Medicare premium was at the highest tier when he turned sixty-five—even though he had had a low income that year. We learned that he sold his business at age sixty-three and that created the high income the premium got based on.

This isn't a permanent increase in Medicare but only for that year, and then it gets recalculated each year moving forward. For example, this client will go back to the lowest tier for Medicare premiums because he had a lower income at age sixty-four.

You also need to be aware of Medicare premiums when doing Roth conversions and other tax-planning strategies that may increase your income today. If you're sixty-three or older, you need to make sure you're accounting for Medicare premiums. They shouldn't scare you and stop you from doing higher amounts of Roth conversions, but they are something you want to keep in mind.

We recommend some people pay more in Medicare premiums to get more to the Roth, while we recommend to other people it isn't worth paying extra in Medicare premiums, and maybe we only go to the top of the first tier. We need to run the numbers.

Also be aware that if you're even a buck over the Medicare premium income tier of $212,000—one dollar!— then you'll pay the higher premium. We had a client who did a Roth conversion on their own, and they were only a few dollars over the tier. Since then, they decided to get help to not make a "stupid" mistake again. Tax planning isn't a DIY calculation nor something you can figure out off the internet to decide if you should convert. You need to do your due diligence and consider the many factors, and we have advanced tools and calculators to show you if this is worthwhile.

# CHAPTER 19

# HOW DOES SOCIAL SECURITY IMPACT YOUR TAXES?

Is Social Security funding going to run out? If you think so, then maybe you should skip this section. I'm only half joking. With the research I've done, I don't think Social Security will run out, but it's certainly in trouble. There's no denying that. The Social Security Administration even admits on its website that its funding is an issue.

## Why Is Social Security in Trouble?

In a nutshell, Social Security is in trouble because the math doesn't add up.

So much has changed since the program started in 1935. Full retirement age was sixty-five, but life expectancy was only sixty-three back then. On average, Social

Security wouldn't have to pay out, and no stress was put on the system.

Today, the full retirement age for Social Security benefits is between sixty-six and sixty-seven. Not much of a difference. The real difference is that today we're seeing people live much longer than sixty-three. Where is the program getting the extra money to pay out the funds?

They're sure not getting it from the people who are working. Back in 1935, there were over forty workers for every retiree. Many more people were paying in than taking out. Today, there are three workers for every retiree—and that number is set to decrease to two to one in the future.

There is an influx of new retirees into the system, and 10,000 baby boomers are turning sixty-five every day.[12] They've been doing so for the last ten years and will continue until 2030.[13]

So why am I telling you *not* to worry? What will the government do to keep Social Security in place? They'll do the same thing today as they did in the 1980s: Make a multitude of changes. In the 1980s Social Security was on the brink of collapse, and they made some changes to keep it in place for a longer period of time.

---

12    https://www.aarpinternational.org/initiatives/aging-readiness-competitiveness-arc/
      united-states

13    https://legaljobs.io/blog/retirement-statistics

Before the 1980s Social Security wasn't taxable. Now, up to 85 percent of your benefit can be taxable. The full retirement age used to be sixty-five, now it's sixty-seven. The program could always tax people who are working more and have the higher-income individuals pay more into Social Security. These are the types of changes they have made and will continue to make to keep the program in place.

One of the things I feel strongly that the Social Security Administration won't do is reduce retirees' benefits. With all the baby boomers at the age of receiving benefits, it would be politically risky to push this issue on the largest generation in our country. My advice to retirees is to expect your benefits to stay about the same. If they go up, that can be considered a bonus.

However, for your children or grandchildren and generations to come? They may be more in trouble. I still think Social Security will be there, but it won't be as generous, for the reasons I've expressed. Educate your children and grandchildren to save wisely—tax-wisely.

## Is Social Security Taxable?

Social Security isn't taxable to everyone nowadays. It isn't taxed to low-income earners, and that entices two types of people: those who are poor and those who are smart. I've already said I definitely don't want you to be poor, so let's talk about how to be smart and how to get your Social Security tax-free.

To see if Social Security is taxed to you, you need to know your provisional income. See the following chart to determine yours. Add the four categories, and you get your provisional income.

| SOCIAL SECURITY TAX | | | |
|---|---|---|---|
| **Provisional Income** | | | |
| 1/2 of Social Security | Ordinary Income | Capital Gains and Dividends | Non Taxable Interest |

1. If you have $40,000 in Social Security, then you'll use $20,000 in the calculation.

2. Ordinary income mainly consists of earned income, tax-deferred investment withdrawals, and pension withdrawals.

3. Capital gains and dividends consist of the investments you have that force you to pay these each year—for example, non-retirement investments, rental properties when sold, and selling a business.

4. Not as many people have non-taxable interest, but for example this could be something like a municipal bond.

Once you have that number, take it to our next chart to find out how much of your Social Security benefit will be taxable.

| TAXATION OF SOCIAL SECURITY BENEFITS | | |
|---|---|---|
| **Filing Status** | **Provisional Income** | **Social Security Subject to Tax** |
| Married Filing Jointly | Under $32,000<br>$32,000-$44,000<br>Over $44,000 | 0<br>Up to 50%<br>Up to 85% |
| Single | Under $25,000<br>$25,000-$34,000<br>Over $34,000 | 0<br>Up to 50%<br>Up to 85% |

Let me give you a few examples of how the preceding chart works if you're married filing jointly. If your provisional income is $30,000, none of your Social Security would be subject to taxes. If your provisional income is $40,000, only 50 percent of the amount above $32,000 would be subject to taxes.

In other words: At $40,000, your provisional income is $8,000 more than $32,000. Fifty percent of that $8,000 would be $4,000, so you would be subject to tax at income rates on that $4,000.

If your provisional income is $50,000, only 50 percent of the amount between $32,000 and $44,000 would be subject to taxes. You would also be crossing into the next bracket of 85 percent, which means 85 percent of the amount above $44,000 would be subject to tax.

In other words: At $50,000, your provisional income would be $18,000 more than $32,000, and $6,000 more than the next level, $44,000. You would be subject to taxes at income rates on $6,000 (50 percent of the amount between $32,000 and $44,000), and on $5,100 (85 percent of the amount over $44,000).

If we add those two numbers together, $6,000 + $5,100 = $11,100, then $11,100 of your Social Security would be subject to income tax.[14]

In this example, to keep things simple, if you had no other income and only lived on Social Security, you would pay $0 in federal income taxes since you would stay under the standard deduction. Living that tax-free retirement— that's what we're talking about!

---

14  You could have $11,100 *subject* to tax, but you still may not *pay* tax on it if that number (plus the rest of your income) is less than the standard deduction.

# FOR THE ANALYTICAL MIND

Congrats for staying with me all the way to chapter 20. I want to state something clearly: My team and I crunch the numbers so you don't have to. We fully understand how complex some of these calculations are. But for those of you with an analytical mind, let's do a deeper dive into efficient tax planning.

The following chart does an excellent job of showing the power of diversification and the importance of timing when taking income from certain assets. The chart shows an analysis we did for a client to show them three options of how they could take out $100,000 a year in retirement. The only difference between the three is where they take that money from. Note that we created this plan in 2023, so it uses 2023 tax brackets. The plans that we create today use current numbers.

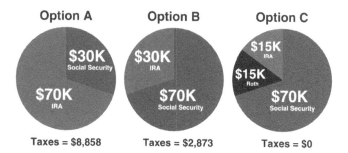

**Option A**     **Option B**     **Option C**

$30K Social Security   $30K IRA   $15K IRA

$70K IRA   $70K Social Security   $15K Roth   $70K Social Security

Taxes = $8,858     Taxes = $2,873     Taxes = $0

## Tax-Efficient Income Planning

Let me explain what's happening here. In this example, the clients needed $100,000 worth of income each year.

In option A, the clients took Social Security at the earliest age and got reduced benefits, so they could only get $30,000 from Social Security. Since they did that, they'll now have to take out $70,000 from their IRA ongoing. They don't have any money in a Roth, so they'll have to pay almost $9,000 in taxes because they're forcing Social Security to be fully taxable, which pushes them into higher federal tax brackets.

In option B, the clients took Social Security at the latest age and received the highest benefit available to them, which was $70,000. Since they did that, they will now only have to take out $30,000 from their IRA ongoing. They still don't have any money in a Roth, so they'll have to pay less than half of what they paid in option A in taxes because they're forcing Social Security to be less taxable and therefore able to keep their tax rate lower. The client also lives in Ohio, which doesn't tax Social Security. So with more of their income coming from Social Security, they'll pay fewer state taxes with only a $30,000 IRA withdrawal versus a $70,000 IRA withdrawal in option A.

In option C, the client took Social Security at the latest age, just like in option B. The big difference in this scenario is that they took out $15,000 from their Roth IRA. Now they'll only have to take out $15,000 from their regular IRA ongoing, and they're able to keep their income under the standard deduction ($27,700), which we learned about earlier. The result: They pay $0 in taxes. And guess what? They may be showing the government they have less than $27,700 and are considered "low income," but they're not living on ramen noodles—they're living on $100,000 a year and enjoying their retirement with fewer concerns about what Uncle Sam will do.

This is a prime example of "It's not how much you make, it's how much you keep." In option A, the client kept $91,142. But in option C, they kept every dollar of their hard-earned $100,000. What would you do with another $9,000 a year in retirement? Sounds to me like a nice family trip with the children and grandchildren. Sounds like a significant impact on your church or charity. Sounds like a lot more peace of mind and a lot less concern about running out of money.

This is how you become "smart" and pay fewer or no taxes over time. Be aware of tax-efficient income planning and don't play games to decide where it's best to take from. Do you really want to flip a coin to see if your retirement is financially successful?

In summary, to be a smart, income tax-free person, you want enough income to maximize the o percent bracket and any lower brackets that could be there now or in the future.

To be clear: This isn't a recommendation for the best time to take your Social Security benefits. We tell clients to take Social Security at all different ages, depending on their specific situation. We are showing a high level of understanding about the impact of where you take out your money and the importance of having tax-efficient income planning. Everything you do with your retirement planning matters. Don't make mistakes from not knowing what to do. Seek help from a professional to make sure you reach the bottom of the "retirement mountain" successfully.

## Your Plan versus the IRS's Plan

Get the IRS out of your life for good. Can you? Sure. After all, if Snoopy[15] can do it, so can you!

---

**Dear IRS,**
I am writing to you to cancel my subscription.
Please remove my name from your mailing list.

---

15    The dog from the late Charles M. Schultz's *Peanuts* comic strip.

How can we make Snoopy's wish come true for you too? We reorganize your finances so that you legally move into the 0 percent tax bracket. We do this for our clients by planning to pay your tax now to allow you to be in a lower tax bracket in the future when it matters most.

The 0 percent tax bracket isn't for everyone. For example, if you have a $50,000-a-year pension, then you'll likely always force yourself over the standard deduction, but it gets you to appreciate the importance of lowering your taxes in your retirement and keeping your income as low as possible. If this is you, then the strategies we're talking about are even more important if you're already starting in the higher brackets and at a disadvantage when it comes to tax planning.

Ready to start planning to live a tax-free retirement?

## The Retiree's Tax Map

Let's tie everything together now. The point we always emphasize with tax planning is everything plays together. You may end up paying more in taxes if you don't know about the "land mines" your increased income could uncover.

As we've emphasized throughout this book, understand that your taxes in retirement are different than the taxes in your working years. Here is a chart from one of our tax-planning software programs that shows how your income in retirement affects not only federal taxes but also many other taxes that are exclusive to retirement.

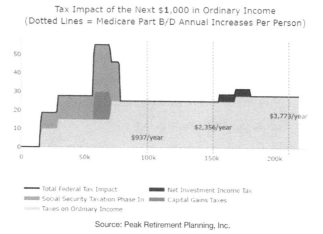

Tax Impact of the Next $1,000 in Ordinary Income
(Dotted Lines = Medicare Part B/D Annual Increases Per Person)

— Total Federal Tax Impact  ▇▇ Net Investment Income Tax
▇▇ Social Security Taxation Phase In  ▇▇ Capital Gains Taxes
▨▨ Taxes on Ordinary Income

Source: Peak Retirement Planning, Inc.

## The Tax Torpedo

The preceding chart represents the "tax torpedo"—when federal taxes, Social Security taxes, and capital gains collide, and you're forced to pay much more in taxes than you expected. The collision forces all three of these to be taxed at a higher level, which could cause you to pay 40 to 50 percent tax on the money on top of that hill.

The torpedo happens because capital gains are at a zero tax bracket until your taxable income reaches the point where you must pay 15 percent. In this instance, our chart shows (in red) someone's increase to the point that they now must pay 15 percent tax on their capital gains. Also, remember that Social Security is 85 percent taxable if your income is higher. You see in the example the full impact of that.

The example shows that if you take out an additional $80,000 from your investments, you'll push your income to that point and dramatically increase the amount you pay Uncle Sam—all because of poor planning. Remember, it isn't as simple as "I'm in the 12 percent tax bracket and only have to pay 12 percent tax." You must remember that there are other factors to consider.

## I Love the Roth, But . . .

By now, you know I love Roth IRAs. However, a Roth IRA doesn't always make sense. An example of when it didn't make sense is when a client of mine was impacted by the tax torpedo.

This is actually a great planning opportunity that you could emulate. Our client was at the top end of the tax torpedo in the example picture. We had a decision to make. Do we want to go over the hill or stay under? If we went over the hill, our client would be allowed to do Roth conversions and get money to the Roth. However, he would be forced to pay a 50 percent tax on about $10,000 for the amount subject to the tax torpedo.

Our client decided to stay under the mountain. To stay under the mountain, we had to do an IRA contribution. Investing in IRAs isn't my favorite strategy with the current tax sale, but at this time, it made sense *not* to pay that 50 percent tax now. Instead, he can defer it down the road when tax rates should be lower for him.

Remember, the key to tax planning is to pay the lowest possible tax allowed without breaking the rules.

## Myth: You Will Be in a Lower Bracket in Retirement

Have you ever been told that you'll be in a lower tax bracket in retirement? If so, then most people with larger tax-deferred investments or pensions and higher Social Security benefits were most likely lied to. To debunk this myth, we wrote another article that also got featured on Kiplinger.com called "Will I Be in a Higher Tax Bracket in Retirement?"[16]

Most people we see in our office will be subject to a higher tax rate in the future. People don't understand this because they forget about Social Security tax and how that impacts them in retirement. You already know how Social Security could be taxable. But if you follow the retiree's tax bracket example we just discussed, you'll realize that if your income pushes Social Security to be taxable, then you're now paying a 12 percent federal tax rate *and* paying tax on Social Security. That means you could be paying a 20 to 30 percent tax rate on the income you take out from your investments or your pension. But remember Social Security doesn't have to be taxable. The only amount of money that's

16    Joe F. Schmitz Jr., CFP®, ChFC®, "Will You Pay Higher Taxes in Retirement?" *Kiplinger*, May 10, 2023, https://www.kiplinger.com/retirement/will-you-pay-higher-taxes-in-retirement.

tax-free is up to your standard or itemized deduction. Anything beyond that may be a higher tax bracket—even if you have a lower income than your working years.

Does it make sense to do a conversion now, even at 22 or 24 percent, knowing you may never be looking at that low a rate again? These are the exact types of conversions we're doing with our clients, which many people don't understand or even consider.

---

**I must emphasize:**
**Just because you're in the 12 percent bracket**
**doesn't mean you're only paying 12 percent tax.**

---

Remember, you can pay those taxes now or later. You've been lied to all your life. The only people who will be paying less tax are those who are poor or have lesser amounts in their tax-deferred investments.

This tax torpedo is such a big issue because the numbers used for calculating Social Security tax (that provisional income that we discussed earlier) haven't been adjusted for inflation since 1985. The time lag and inflation have caused most people to fall into the tax torpedo trap as their income is worth much more than the 1985 value.

This false belief is what we call a "stealth tax." Stealth taxes aren't noticed by the common eye. They gradually creep up and cause you to pay more taxes over time, and they allow the government to get more money from you without telling you. Stealth taxes occur when inflation happens, but brackets and limits are not adjusted to reflect their new inflated value. The Social Security provisional income is an example of a stealth tax since it hasn't been changed since 1985. Net investment income is another one that hasn't changed recently. Other stealth taxes consist of the widow's penalty, the home sale tax exclusion not increasing in recent times, and the ten-year RMD for non-spouse beneficiaries.

How do you plan for stealth taxes? Tax planning and making sure your income is lower in the future so that you have more control and own your retirement.

## How Much Can You Really Save with Tax Planning?

To show the amount of tax savings you could have over your lifetime, we created a proprietary tax calculator from scratch. Our clients love this, and it helps them feel more confident about the tax strategies we implement each year. Every decision we make at Peak Retirement Planning, Inc. is research based. We conduct an analysis and build reports on all the decisions we make. We don't throw darts and hope they land on the right decision.

Let's walk you through what our proprietary tax calculator can do. Here is a real-life example of one of our clients.

## CLIENT DETAILS

| Name | Example |
| --- | --- |
| Age | 60 |
| Tax-Deferred $ Today | $157,000 |
| Annual Growth Rate | 5.00% |
| Tax Rate | 18% |

## CURRENT PLAN

| | |
| --- | --- |
| Taxes Paid on RMDs | $46,130 |
| Taxes Paid on Reinvestment (Cap Gains) | $19,295 |
| Social Security Taxes | $42,672 |
| Taxes Paid by Beneficiaries | $68,863 |
| **Total Taxes Paid** | **$176,960** |

## TAX PLANNING

| | |
| --- | --- |
| Taxes Paid on Conversion | $28,840 |
| Taxes Paid on Growth | - |
| Medicare Premium Increase | - |
| Taxes Paid by Beneficiaries | - |
| **Total Taxes Paid** | **$28,840** |

**Estimated Tax Savings over Lifetime:**

**$148,120**

We're showing some high-level numbers here for illustrative purposes to show you the impact of tax planning. The far left column shows assumptions. We ran this for a joint couple who were sixty years old. They had over $1 million in tax-deferred assets, but we were trying to decide what we should do for this year, so that's where the $157,000 comes from.

After we ran their numbers in our other tax software applications, we learned that a Roth conversion for that amount would maximize their ending net worth during their lifetime. Since they're conservative investors, we assumed a 5 percent growth rate. The effective tax rate of 18 percent is what they would pay this year to convert the $157,000 to a Roth. As you can see in the far right column, our clients would have to pay $28,840 in taxes to do that. You're thinking, that's a lot of money. Yes, it is, but not comparatively, as I'll show you. If they do this Roth conversion now, they'll pay no more tax ongoing on that money.

Let's look at the middle section, "Current Plan". These are the numbers our clients are looking at if they did nothing—what I call the IRS's plan. In this scenario, they'll have to pay taxes on their RMD every year, a total of $46,130 over their lifetime (assuming a 25 percent tax rate, this percentage could be more, as we've discussed). In their situation, they didn't want to take their RMDs because they had no need for them. If they were to take those out and reinvest them, then the gain would be taxable at capital gains rates on any of the growth ongoing, which we estimate to be $19,295. With this RMD, they would be forcing themselves into the Social Security tax torpedo, causing them to pay an extra $42,672 in Social Security taxes over their lifetime. Their beneficiaries would have to pay taxes over ten years on this money, amounting to $68,863 in taxes due.

The total taxes over our clients' lifetime adds up to $176,961. That's a lot of taxes. It's hard to believe they could pay more in taxes than what the investment is worth today. The good news? They don't have to pay that much in taxes. By having a plan, they could save $148,120.

---

### What could an extra $148,120 mean for you in retirement?

---

# CHAPTER 21

# PEAK RETIREMENT FOR YOU

There's a specific reason our firm's name is Peak Retirement Planning, Inc. The name "Peak" comes from the following mountain graphic. The purpose of what we do is to help people in or near retirement get down the mountain safely in retirement and navigate the risks.

## The Retirement Mountain

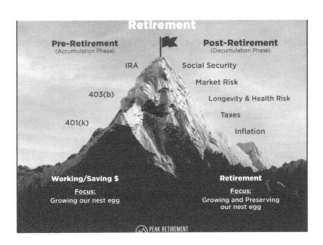

The retirement mountain graphic shows you that you need strategies not only to climb to the top of the mountain from the pre-retirement side, but to skillfully make your way down the post-retirement side. The point of the graphic is to emphasize that planning for retirement isn't as easy as planning during your working years.

As you've learned, during your working years, you're really only worried about the taxes on your income from your paycheck. You're climbing up the retirement mountain so focused on saving that you don't see the tax bill looming on the other slope.

When you reach retirement, things get a bit complex, and the following questions will arise:

- Where will you get money or withdraw money from to replace that income you no longer have coming in?
- What is the tax impact of taking money out of different investments?
- How does Social Security affect your tax situation?
- What if the market is down when you need your money?

There are many new details to be aware of in retirement. One mistake could be costly. Think about it: All your life you've worked hard and saved as much as you can for this moment. Is it enough? If it is enough, then are you maximizing it and making sure you're not missing tax savings and smart investment opportunities?

I would like you to believe that this type of retirement financial planning is important enough for you to spend extra time on to make sure you're on track. My team is here to help you understand your current financial situation *and* what it could look like in ten or twenty years from today if 1) you take no new actions and 2) you take smart actions to reduce your lifetime tax burden.

I'll share an interesting story from a gentleman who attended one of our retirement workshops and gave me my favorite quote ever. He came up to me afterward and pointed to the retirement mountain.

"This mountain right here is the best thing you talked about tonight," he said. "I'm right here on the way down, three years into retirement, and I've realized planning is a lot harder than I thought."

The man told me he checks the stock market while on vacation and reads a hundred pages of tax law changes every year. Then he said the best thing I may have ever heard: "I don't want to make a stupid mistake where I have to go back to work or put my retirement for me and my wife in jeopardy. I need help."

To his point, if you've worked for thirty or forty-five years for retirement, then I think taking a few hours to meet with a professional and making sure everything is in the best shape possible is well worth the time.

## Advisors and Tax Planners: How We Are Different from Them

So many advisors don't talk about tax planning. How do you know if yours does? Well, consider how they are doing with this checklist:

- Has your advisor ever reviewed your tax return? When was the last review?
- Does your advisor prep your taxes?
- Have they helped you with tax strategies in the last five years?
- Have they built you a long-range tax plan? Is it one that covers the coming twenty years, fewer years, more years?
- Have they explained the impact your investments have today and what the tax ramifications will be in the future?
- Have they calculated and helped plan for your Required Minimum Distributions?
- Have they discussed the impacts you may have with IRMAA and Social Security tax?
- Do they use software to analyze your taxes?

- Have they suggested a Roth IRA or Roth conversion?

- Are they an insurance salesperson, investment manager, or a comprehensive retirement planner? (Do you even know?)

It really bothers me when I see advisors charge high fees and fail to deliver high-level services. It makes our industry and profession look less dependable. Financial planners have such an important level of trust from clients, and it's our obligation to give them excellent service that goes the extra mile. This is one of the reasons I started Peak Retirement Planning, Inc., to give retirees the experience they deserve when working with financial planners.

If your advisor hasn't brought these topics to you, then I would frankly *not* recommend that you go back to them—and certainly not to ask them for help with what you've learned in these pages. They won't know how to help. Remember, you're paying them for advice, not paying them to implement ideas you've brought to them. What are you paying them for if they're not being proactive for you?

At this point in your life, you don't need the family doctor. You need a team of tax-planning specialists whose focus is comprehensive, low-tax/no-tax retirement planning. You want the cardiologist of financial planning.

But you also need a team and not an individual. You want a team of specialists who keeps up with the legislative changes to the US Tax Code and with how the code particularly affects a retiree. You want a team of specialists to bring the ideas to you, not simply comment "good or not good" to the strategies you're currently employing.

At Peak Retirement Planning, Inc., we believe it is ultra important to have the CPA team and the CERTIFIED FINANCIAL PLANNER™ team working together with our clients. That is why we offer tax prep for our clients in-house. This allows us to ensure all of the advanced tax planning strategies we recommend get implemented when filing taxes. This is not common for financial planning firms to do, but we highly recommend you work with a team that does all of the tax planning and prep in-house. We also recommend you choose a firm that offers estate planning in-house. Having all three professionals in one place allows you to not miss anything and have a complete plan.

I once worked with a CPA who wasn't bringing new ideas to the table and wasn't adding value for the fee I was paying. I found another CPA who had new ideas and added instant value for my needs. My former CPA—who I had worked with for almost five years—never brought up such ideas. What do you think I did? Of course, I went with the new CPA. I didn't hesitate one second. I sprinted to get her advice, and I consult her now quite frequently and regularly.

I realize that your advisor may have become your friend, and you may have worked with this person for twenty years. But your retirement isn't about loyalty—you're making a business decision. Every decision you make in retirement must lead to paying only the taxes you owe and not a penny more on your hard-earned life savings.

## Why Don't Advisors Talk about Tax Planning?

So why don't other professionals talk about tax planning? There are many reasons.

### Liability

Many of the bigger companies in our industry won't allow their advisors to talk about many of the tax strategies we put on the table for our clients. Straight-up forbids them. Those companies shall remain nameless, but don't believe for a minute that I'm protecting them.

These national or larger firms may have hired less-experienced advisors. Their compliance department must set boundaries since the liability is on the company if an advisor gives incorrect tax advice. Bigger companies would have to take more of the burden rather than the advisor, so they flat-out prohibit certain topics and strategies from being discussed.

### Expertise

Expertise in our industry is marked by a credential: Certified Financial Planner, the CFP® credential. While all investment advisors are supposed to act in the client's best interest, if advisors who have earned the CFP® credential designation fail to act in the client's best interest, they can lose the certification. It requires passing a rigorous education program and certification exam to receive the designation.

In training programs, advisors spend over six thousand hours developing holistic financial plans for a range of real-world challenges. There is a tax course in this training. This is important to understand because not every financial advisor is a CFP®. They may not have the training to recognize these strategic opportunities and advise on them.

If an advisor doesn't have their CFP® or isn't in training to get it, then how serious are they about maximizing your life savings?

### Continuing Education

Taxes are written in pencil and change every day. You must spend time reading new rules and strategies every day. Most advisors were trained to sell investment and insurance products and not to do comprehensive retirement planning.

*Time*

To be frank, most advisors don't want to take the time to learn the ins and outs of taxes (even the basics, and let's not talk about most advisors' ignorance about more advanced strategies). When they have over five hundred clients, they can't and don't spend the time to do this intensive learning either. Sad, but true.

*Compensation*

You'll find this ludicrous but easy to understand. Some advisors won't advise on tax strategies because they'll get paid less. For example, if you do a Roth conversion, you must take money out to pay the taxes today, as I've explained. This means the advisor will now have less of your money to manage, and they'll ultimately get paid less in fees and commissions. They would not only be doing additional work to advise you on advanced strategies but also be getting paid less in the process. I've actually had other advisors tell me this.

## What about CPAs?

You may wonder, why is your own CPA not talking about this? CPAs don't specialize in this specific area.

Listen, I love CPAs, and they're good at what they do: tax *preparation*. They don't do tax *planning*. They work your past numbers, while your retirement tax planning requires us to look at your future numbers. In other words, CPAs are reactive and not proactive. I have a CPA, even with all my tax expertise. Why? They do different work than what we're talking about.

Most CPAs don't know your full situation. They don't ask for your total net worth and retirement goals. They only file the documents you give them at the end of the year to make sure they're reported correctly. Their biggest goal is to help you pay less tax *today*, while ours is to help you pay much less tax over your lifetime.

We even have many clients who are CPAs who work with us to get help with the strategies we mentioned in this book.

### To Summarize

I know I'm speaking ill of our industry, and I don't say it to discourage you from working with a professional. I say it to make sure you're working with the right team and to give you the knowledge to know what you're looking for. There are great financial planners out there, and I recommend most people to work with someone.

### All about AJ

My nephew, AJ, was born on November 5, 2019. On no birthday since then have I ever given him a physical gift.

---
### Instead, I put money toward an investment for him.
---

Do you think he understands the value of an investment at his age? Of course not. So he may not like me as much right now—I'm "that" uncle.

However, how do you think he'll feel about me in twenty years when he does see the value of the investment? How will he feel about my gift when it provides him the money to start a business, or help with a down payment on a house, or buy a car, or even take his ol' Uncle Joe out for a steak dinner?

You're right. We'll be best friends, and I'll leave a lifetime impact on him about the value of saving and investing.

The look my nephew gives me now when he gets no gifts.

The look my nephew will give me in twenty years (after he buys me a steak dinner).

This story about AJ is similar to the way you need to think about this book. These strategies—the basic ones and the advanced ones—may leave you confused and unsure how to confidently implement them. That's why you need professional assistance and to think long term, like I am for AJ. Think about the impact these strategies can have on helping you reduce your lifetime tax bill. For some of our clients, the savings are in the multiple six figures or for some, even in the seven figures, but for most the savings will be at least $100,000 (savings that don't go to "that" uncle, Uncle Sam).

Implementing these strategies will also give you peace of mind in retirement. You'll know that you've maximized your lifetime earnings, kept as much as legally possible, and paid your legally required taxes (and not a penny more). What you've worked so hard to accumulate over your lifetime is truly yours.

I want you to picture how good it will feel to have all your affairs in order in this manner.

I want you to picture how good it will feel to live the retirement you dream of.

I want you to picture how good it will feel to have hundreds of thousands of dollars *extra* in your retirement account, even though it was yours all along, because you took the time to understand the rules and get help from a professional.

I want you to picture how good it will feel to not worry about money, to do what you want, when you want, with who you want—traveling, spending time with grandchildren, supporting your church or charities, buying new things with no real worry about the price tags.

The great news is you have the control and the time to do this. It's all up to you to make the decision about how you want your future to look.

As I've mentioned, doing nothing is doing something. Inaction is the worst thing you can do. So, although I said you have the time to do this, don't wait. I can't stand it when people are lazy and don't take needed action. It wasn't how I was raised. My dad is the hardest worker I know. I've worked with him since I was five years old.

One of the lessons he taught me over the years is that if you want something, you must go get it. No handouts. Don't be a victim and say you hate paying taxes and then sit and do nothing. Act. Do something about it.

You are responsible for your financial life, and if you don't get professional help, you could be settling for a lesser retirement. Why work so hard and not preserve every dime of your earnings? Take control, own your retirement, and get Uncle Sam out of your pocket.

Your future self will thank you.

## Your No. 1 Basic Rule:
## Get Professional Assistance

The biggest point I want to make—and the one thing I want you to take from this book—is to get professional assistance. Whether you want to set the basics correctly in place or you want to choose the right advanced strategy or strategies for your circumstances, get expert help.

Get help from a trusted team of fiduciaries who know how to manage your investments and bring a comprehensive tax focus to your retirement planning. The generalist—the family doctor—won't suffice anymore. You're at a point when you need a specialist.

It's never too late to do some serious tax planning and consider advanced strategies. But not all the strategies we present are appropriate to all our clients, so that's why sitting down with our team will be the best way you could spend an hour this year. We'll be able to determine the strategies that are best for you.

---

**Divorcing Uncle Sam can be done. It has been done. My guess is that you could do it too.**

---

Retirement planning with a tax focus isn't something everyone can do. We specialize in it, and we do it every day. If you're looking for guidance, feel free to reach out to us. At Peak Retirement Planning, Inc., we take a team approach because your retirement shouldn't be left in the hands of one person. I've trained my team in an intensive and extensive training program about how to maximize people's retirements. All our advisors are fully licensed fiduciaries and either have their CFP® or are in the process of getting their CFP®. We're excited to help those in or near retirement make sure they're getting the most out of their hard-earned life savings.

**Apply to talk with Peak Retirement Planning, Inc. at**
***PeakRetirementPlanning.com.***

Remember, it's not how much money you make. Not by a long shot. It's how much you keep that counts.

And remember this quote from George Sutherland: "The legal right of a taxpayer to decrease the amount of what otherwise would be his taxes, or altogether avoid them, by means which the law permits, cannot be doubted."

Let's get planning.

A SNEAK PREVIEW OF

## *MIDWESTERN MILLIONAIRE*

# ①

# THE TRAITS OF A
# MIDWESTERN MILLIONAIRE

Let me be clear about the Midwestern Millionaire. This isn't about American geography. You don't have to live in the Midwest to be a Midwestern Millionaire. We work with people living all across the country, and many of our clients who live on the East or West Coast and down South meet these criteria and have the same values as Midwesterners.

The following list outlines eight of the key traits we see in the Midwestern Millionaire:

### 1. Diligent Saver

As mentioned, the Midwestern Millionaire has saved at least $1 million. This is no easy accomplishment, considering all the things life can throw at you over the years. They have done this by being . . .

## 2. Frugal

Midwestern Millionaires are great savers and the worst spenders. That's how I like to explain it. It is that pair of "money habits" that has allowed them to accumulate their wealth.

They often like saving money on ordinary purchases, and they're content without having the most luxurious items. They're frugal; it's second nature to them. If they find blueberries on sale at the store, they stock up. At the end of this chapter, I'll tell a funny story about blueberries to emphasize this trait, which goes hand-in-hand with . . .

## 3. Hardworking

Midwestern Millionaires are willing to do whatever it takes, however long it takes. They are conscientious and consistent workers. They put their head down and get things done. My parents are two of the hardest workers I know and couldn't be better examples of Midwestern Millionaires.

My dad taught me that the day isn't over until the job is done. My mom taught me that you must give 100 percent in everything you do, often saying, "How you do anything is how you do everything."

They do everything needed because as Midwestern Millionaires, they . . .

### 4. Want to Pay Less in Taxes

They believe their hard-earned income and their life savings should be in their pockets and not in Uncle Sam's. They never want to overpay in taxes. Now, they're not against paying taxes, but they only want to pay their fair share and not "tip" Uncle Sam anything extra. They believe the government isn't necessarily the best steward of their taxpaying dollars. They believe in lowering taxes to allow for "We the People" to have more control over the economy, as opposed to giving more to the government and allowing them to control how our money is spent. People with Midwestern values also typically don't believe in handouts; they believe what you get is earned and not given.

The more money you have, the more tax you pay. Midwestern Millionaires know they will pay lots of taxes over their retirement unless they start successfully implementing tax-planning strategies now. They're also . . .

### 5. Risk-Averse

They want to protect their savings. Midwestern Millionaires are more conservative in their investing approach and want to find investments that are less aggressive and more stable and consistent over time. Yes, they want a return, but they don't want to take on more risk than they need to. They may want to achieve single and doubles now instead of swinging for the faces.

They also want to protect their wealth from health-care bills (they've heard or seen how medical costs can be extremely costly throughout retirement). They strive to ensure that their wealth will transfer to their spouse and children without losing any of that wealth. They don't want to miss anything. This proves they are also . . .

### 6. Family Oriented

Family is extremely important to Midwestern Millionaires. I've always been told to take care of those who take care of me. Likewise, many of our clients truly care about making sure their family is taken care of.

Our clients want their spouse to be taken care of when they pass away, and they want their kids and grandkids to have the opportunities and resources that will set them up for success. We can help them build financial plans that prepare for the loss of a spouse and build generational wealth for their families in the future.

One way we do this is through advanced tax planning. Midwestern Millionaires love learning about and imple-menting strategies that will ensure their family gets more of their wealth than Uncle Sam. We also do smart estate planning using strategies that allow the smooth transfer of assets to the next generation. We see that as not only having estate documents (which are extremely important) but also by having a rock-solid estate plan that incorporates advanced tax planning and purpose.

Midwestern Millionaires know they are blessed with wealth, but they remain . . .

## 7. Humble

You would never know the Midwestern Millionaire is a millionaire and has had extreme success over their lifetime. They don't always drive a flashy car or live in the biggest house. They don't participate in the latest fashion trends or spend thousands of dollars on clothing. One of our clients wears the same shirt nearly every time we see him (yes, it's washed). It's an Old Navy shirt from twenty years ago with an American flag on it. Is he still wearing it because he can't afford a new shirt? No, he wears it because he is content with what he has and is not trying to impress others with new fancy clothing. He even says, "They don't make shirts like they used to." He has bought a product of quality from a manufacturer he believes shares his own commitment to being . . .

## 8. Trusting and Trustworthy

Because the needed planning is so complex, many Midwestern Millionaires work with a team as they prepare for retirement and work through retirement. This means they trust a team to help manage what they have worked so hard to accumulate for the last forty years. That kind of trust is important, especially when the team might not understand how much this means to you and how much you have sacrificed to get to where you are.

Integrity is one of the most essential qualities a financial planning team must have when managing someone's life savings. You must find out if the advisory team you decide to work with has integrity. Ask the right questions, research the company, and search the team's personal social media pages (to see who they are when they're not in a suit and what they do when no one is watching). "How you do anything is how you do everything." This is your life savings, so who you trust to help you with it is a big decision.

Now, as promised, I will present my story about blueberries, which illustrates the Midwestern Millionaire's character traits very well.

## Frozen Blueberries

I was at my parents' house one day and happened to open their deep freezer. After staring unbelievingly for half a minute, I realized the entire freezer chest was full of blueberries. The whole thing!

I asked my mother why she would do something like this, and she said: "Because they were on sale."

I definitely understand that "sale" concept. I'm the same way (family trait—the apple didn't fall far from the tree). I buy items on sale and save money when I can, because I work hard for my money, and I value it. I still had to challenge my mom, however, and press her for more information. She's in a great financial situation and wouldn't be set back by buying blueberries at full price (even in the quantity filling her freezer).

"It's the principle of the matter," she explained.

It's what she was taught throughout her years growing up. My mom came from a bigger family and was taught how to be frugal and to wisely preserve and conserve what she had. She has carried that mindset with her throughout her life. Just like almost every Midwestern Millionaire, she is naturally frugal.

What I have found after a lifetime of observing my mother's behaviors, traits, and values is that this type of money-saving purchase gives her joy. To save money on something she would have bought anyway delights her— like she's won. It is, in fact, the principle of the matter to her: Even though she can buy the blueberries at full price and not hurt financially because of it, she would rather save the money and consider it a win in her books for being frugal. I'm sure many of you reading this book share this trait.

This is the kind of Midwestern Millionaire care, attention, and diligence you want to deploy when it comes to managing and maximizing your life savings. It's the kind of attention and care we deploy for each client. That's why we work with those with Midwestern values, just like us.

Back to my mom for a moment. Sometimes I try not to encourage my mom about how well she's doing because she currently works with us at Peak Retirement Planning, Inc. as my Executive Assistant. It's a job she's good at and has experience with. She worked for the federal government in Columbus, Ohio for the top executives at the Defense Logistics Agency, which is a big deal. Here's the thing: I can't let her think she could retire, or I would lose a key employee. I'm joking, of course. I seriously love working with my mom. She quit her job to help me start this firm when I was twenty-five years old. That means the world to me.

People often ask what it's like working with my mom, and I tell them it's nothing new. She has been my assistant and been there for me all my life. Although she could retire, she enjoys the purpose of our mission that we have and is dedicated to serving others. Many Midwestern Millionaires also share that trait of wanting to have a purpose throughout all their years, including retirement.

Now, let's dive into the care, attention, and diligence that is needed and what Midwestern Millionaires must do now with their life savings to protect it.

# RESOURCES FROM
## PEAK RETIREMENT PLANNING, INC.

## READ

Read our Amazon bestselling books, "I Hate Taxes" and "Midwestern Millionaire".

Browse our articles that are featured in National Kiplinger publications for financial tips and more!

**KIPLINGER**

## WATCH

Watch us weekly on the news where we discuss important retirement strategies.

Find us on YouTube, where we publish educational videos for those in or near retirement every week!

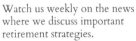

**YOUTUBE**

## LISTEN

Listen online or on the radio to hear us discuss your top retirement concerns.

Tune in to our educational podcast "Joe Knows Retirement."

**PODCAST**

**www.peakretirementplanning.com | info@peakretirementplanning.com**

# ABOUT THE AUTHOR

Joe F. Schmitz Jr., CFP®, ChFC®, CKA® is the owner of Peak Retirement Planning, Inc. based in Columbus, Ohio.

Joe has built a comprehensive retirement planning firm focused on helping clients grow and preserve their wealth. Under Joe's leadership, a team of experienced financial advisors use tax-efficient strategies, investment management, income planning, health-care planning, and estate planning to help clients feel confident in their financial future—and the legacy they leave behind.

As a CERTIFIED FINANCIAL PLANNER™, Joe has passed a rigorous education program and certification exam to receive the CFP® designation, and he also has well over the six thousand hours of professional experience required by the CFP®. What's more, Joe has received the designation of Certified Kingdom Advisor®, demonstrating that he has learned the finer points of retirement planning, investing, insurance, and taxation in accord with Christian principles. He has created a firm that helps his clients have a deep sense of purpose in how they steward their wealth.

Joe got his start in the financial services industry in 2015. He graduated with a bachelor of science in finance and financial planning from Mount Vernon Nazarene University, where he played basketball and ran track. He has lived near Columbus his entire life.

When Joe isn't in the office, he can be found running, hiking, biking, or reading. He also enjoys traveling and spending time with family and friends. In addition, Joe sponsors and coaches a youth basketball team for Nova Village Athletic Club.

Made in United States
Cleveland, OH
21 December 2025

29690129R00111